To: "URSULA"

"THE PURPOSE OF LIFE"

IS

"A LIFE WITH PURPOSE!"

Ebbie

MAY 17 - 2023

A Memoire

AMERICAN BY CHOICE

EBERHARD L. BULACH

Photographs and Documents
All photographs and documents come from the family albums of the Bulach family.

 Second Edition, May 2015;
Third Edition, September 2020; Fourth Edition, September 2022
Printed in the United States of America
ISBN: 9781633187665
www.TheBookPatch.com

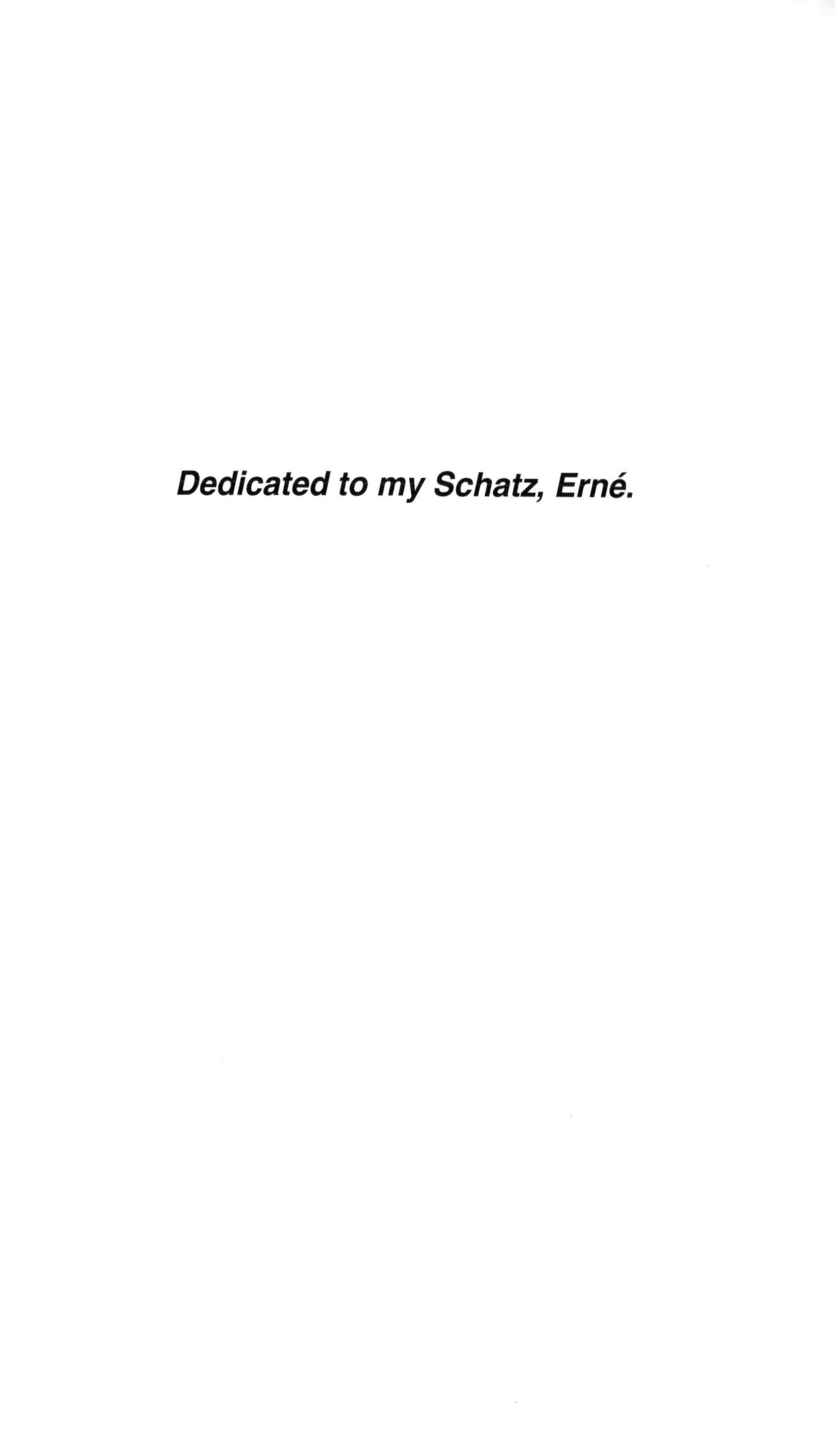

Dedicated to my Schatz, Erné.

PROLOGUE

My motivation in writing this memoir comes out of gratitude for the many people who have loved, mentored and supported me throughout my life. I also wish to leave a legacy, both personal and historical, for my children and grandchildren. I am deeply grateful for the freedom of opportunity I have experienced and I follow closely the current political discussions on immigration reform in the United States.

The stringent and well-organized social system I experienced in 1951 has become a national disaster. I was an immigrant to the United States seeking opportunity and eager to make a positive contribution to this great country. I have never filed for unemployment or asked for Public Assistance. I was always expected to assimilate into the American culture and even register for the military draft. Nowhere, but in American could I have enjoyed the opportunity to build a successful business, live where I choose, build a home and return a portion of my wealth to the community and people in need. I am grateful and humbled by this ability.

I cannot help but feel a deep sense of gratitude for all that Uncle Gene and Aunt Florence Bulach did for me. They treated me like a son and provided opportunities that many children did not have; especially a young boy from war torn Germany. Their generosity I can repay only by living my life in such a way that I express their selfless giving through my own actions among family, friends and strangers.

To my ***Schatz*** (treasure) and wife of 54 years, Erné - I am blessed beyond measure for your support, confidence and trust along our life's journey. You stood by me when I strayed from the logical path to take an alternative route that didn't always turn out as expected.

To my children, Steve and Tina – You have grown into remarkable individuals and successful business owners through your fortitude and ambition. You are devoted and responsible parents. I am extremely proud of you both.

To my grandchildren, Dakkota, Tommy, Margarete, Max and Spencer – Oma and I follow your development, school activities and career choices with great interest wondering where life will direct your paths.

To my devoted siblings – Thank you for your constant support and interest in my life throughout the years. You welcome and accept me always as if I never left Germany.

To my loyal, treasured friends and business associates – Thank you for standing by me through thick and thin; in good times and in challenging times. ***Zum Wohl!***

To my team who made this book a reality: Elizabeth Horsager, my friend and editor-in-chief; Emily Erickson, my trusty assistant, who copied, printed and emailed information throughout the editing process; Linda Schwarz, my niece and cover designer, who again connects Germany and Minnesota; Clovis Brackins, my friend, who encouraged me to write my story and read the initial draft; Evelyn Klein, the voice of experience, who offered many tips on formal writing and publishing.

Vielen Dank!
Ebbie
April 2014

❖

I have always been a baseball fan and still enjoy watching a good game on TV, in spite of the limitations placed upon us all during the current COVID-19 pandemic. As Erné and I are rounding third base on our life's journey, we reflect on the amazing experiences we have had in living out our 'American Dream'. Our fellow travelers along the way have offered us friendship, companionship and support. Some people entered briefly and vanished. Others lingered a bit longer. However, many people held on for the duration of the ride. Together, we all created great memories and the love we received left big footprints on our hearts.

We've reached two more milestones during the year 2020, Erné's 80th birthday and our 60th wedding anniversary. I hope that we reach our eternal home without the need to slide into home plate.

Erné, my sunshine and soul mate, and I left our native Germany and our families in search of a place to call home: our own promised land. Generations before us did the same thing and we followed in their footsteps. We are extremely grateful to God, the Almighty, for granting us the privilege to experience freedom and happiness in, what I consider, the greatest country in the world.

Thank you fellow pilgrims for joining us in this dream.

Ebbie
August 2020

FROM THE EDITOR

Over the years, Eberhard and his friends have certainly entered into many conversations regarding their individual and collective immigration experiences and life. Ebbie credits his good friend, Clovis Brackins, for encouraging him to write down his memories and stories to eventually take the form of a book. Now, after several years of remembering and writing, the stories that filled a 3-ring binder 3 inches thick have now become this book.

When I heard that Ebbie was looking for an editor, I wanted to help write his story as a way of honoring him and the entire Bulach family for their faithful friendship to me over the past 33 years.

My husband, Kent, and I came to St. Paul, Minnesota as young newlyweds after spending a year in Germany as students. We came to St. Paul's United Church of Christ one Sunday morning in the Fall of 1987, met Erné and Ebbie, and began a life-long friendship that brought together our interests of family, church, Germany and other shared values.

We have enjoyed delicious German meals and desserts in the Bulach home, experienced Oktoberfest at the Gasthaus in Stillwater, participated in the German Karfreitag and Advent worship services, been welcomed warmly by Bulach friends and extended family, and been fortunate to celebrate milestone birthdays, weddings and anniversaries together.

The memories retold here are Eberhard's, but the life journey is really that of Erné and Ebbie, two wonderful, loving and generous individuals. It is my absolute privilege to present this memoir.

With much love and admiration,
Elizabeth Horsager, Editor
St. Paul, August 2020

America[1]

by Neil Diamond

Far, We've been traveling far, Without a home,
But not without a star
Free, Only want to be free
We huddle close, Hang on to a dream
On the boats and on the planes
They're coming to America
Never looking back again, They're coming to America

Home
Don't it seem so far away
Oh, we're traveling light today
In the eye of the storm, In the eye of the storm
Home, To a new and a shiny place
Make our bed and we'll say our grace
Freedom's light burning warm, Freedom's light burning warm
Everywhere around the world, They're coming to America
Ev'ry time that flag's unfurled, They're coming to America

Got a dream to take them there
They're coming to America
Got a dream they've come to share,
They're coming to America, They're coming to America
They're coming to America, They're coming to America, They're coming to America
Today, Today, Today, Today, Today
My country 'tis of thee (today)
Sweet land of liberty (today)
Of thee I sing (today)
Of thee I sing
Today, Today, Today, Today, today, today......

BULACH FAMILY

April 2014

Top Row: Margarete Martin, Dakkota Troy, Tina Bulach, Tommy Bulach
Middle Row: Spencer Martin, Erné Bulach, Eberhard Bulach
Front Row: Steve Bulach, Max Bulach, Beth Bulach

CHAPTER 1

EARLY CHILDHOOD

"Das Wichtigste ist, daß man nicht aufhört zu fragen." ~ Albert Einstein

The most important thing is, one must never stop asking questions.

When I was 5 years old in 1939, I entered kindergarten. The kindergarten classes were held in the ***Gemeindehaus*** (community center) near the Evangelical Church and class was conducted from 9:00 a.m. until 1:00 p.m. We walked from our house to and from the ***Kinderschule***. Else Walker, my next-door neighbor, was my age, my playmate and my school walking companion. At our house, my parents had yard jobs waiting for me after school and on Saturdays. Else's father was a vegetable farmer and always had a job or two for a 5 year old as well.

My very first teacher in kindergarten was ***Schwester Hedwig*** (Sister Hedwig) from a Protestant nun's order. She and two other nuns lived on the second floor of the Gemeindehaus. Not only were the nuns teachers, they were also nurses. If we children had a cut, fever or other minor injury, we would see them first before going to the doctor. Sister Hedwig was very tall and beautiful with dark blue eyes. She was a strict, but fair disciplinarian. To me she was the perfect model of a teacher. Her presence and demeanor commanded respect. She seldom raised her voice or spanked us. We knew she meant business and we got to work just by looking at her facial expression.

My mother was my greatest childhood role model for both men and women. However, Sister Hedwig comes in a very close second place.

Sundays were reserved for the family. We would always go to church in the morning and Sunday dinner was the biggest, best and most important meal of the week. After the meal, we would play or go for long walks in the woods with our parents. The only work done on Sundays was feeding the chickens and picking the eggs. Otherwise, we observed the Lord's Day by resting.

My scariest experience as a very young child was the time I was in the field planting potatoes in the spring with my godfather, Ludwig Hertfelder (my mother's brother), my aunt, my mother and two of my cousins. Our duties, as children, were to help weed the ground around the new potato seeds.

We noticed that the sky was darkening in the west and quickly changing colors from black to dark blue and then to dark green. Uncle Ludwig said we should pack up and leave for home immediately in order to beat the storm. Two cows pulled our 4-wheeled wagon. The adults sat on a board about 2 feet above the wagon bed and we children sat on the floor behind them. It started to thunder and the lightning flashed at close intervals and the clouds moved in quickly. Before we were halfway home, it started to rain. My cousins and I slid underneath the board where the adults sat. We hoped that would protect us from the rain and lightening. We were soon in the midst of a thunderstorm, the likes of which I had never seen. I was overcome with an intense fear and began to cry because the noise was so loud and the storm was so powerful. I thought the world was coming to an end.

I turned to my mother and my Uncle Ludwig. He laughed and tried to reassure me that there was nothing to fear, the storm would pass in about 15 minutes. "You'll just get soaked to your bones," he said. That was the longest 15 minutes of my life and we were, indeed, soaked. I felt embarrassed as my cousins had experienced such a storm before and knew what to expect, but I did not.

I have pleasant memories of summer days working in the fields (hay, wheat, oats, barley - both planting and harvesting). Although we were not old enough to manage the difficult work like the adults, we children always came along to take care of the occasional odd or easy job and to be within eyesight of our parents.

The best part about fieldwork was the lunch or sandwich break. The women filled picnic baskets with round loaves of homemade bread, cheese and sausages. The loaves measured 14-16 inches in diameter and up to 6 inches thick, with a weight of 4-5 pounds. Usually it was the men who cut off the portions of bread. The men also cut portions of the sausage, cheese and butter and divided the other items for the meal. There were no seconds or extra helpings. You ate whatever was given to you and that was it.

Beverages consisted of strong and potent apple cider for the adults and mineral water for the children. The cider was brought along in 5-liter earthen jugs. The jugs were passed along from person to person since we rarely had individual glasses to drink from. On occasion, we children were allowed a drink of the cider. It gave us all kinds of energy until the alcohol wore off and then we laid in the shade to rest.

Since we didn't have coolers or ice cubes, the jugs were placed in a nearby creek and covered with a wet cloth. Sometimes the creek was some distance from the work place. This is when the children had work to do. Whenever someone was thirsty, one of us would go to the creek to fetch the jug. There were times when we would return the jugs to the creek without paying attention to where we placed them. Then we would have to look for them again. On extremely hot days, it was easy to run out of cider. When that happened, one of the children had to go home and refill the jug. Carrying the empty jug was tough as it was quite heavy. Carrying back the full jug was quite a chore, especially if home was almost one mile away.

My father seldom came along to the fields because he was a streetcar driver and conductor. His work came in shifts sometimes starting at 3:30 a.m. and ending at 12:00 noon or starting at 4:00 p.m. and ending after midnight. His work schedule included weekends as well.

Father's free time was spent working in our large yard planting or pruning trees, cutting grass, weeding and harvesting fruit. However, he did love to travel. And as an employee of the streetcar company, he periodically received free passes from the railroad for the entire family. Mother didn't like to travel, though. She was a homebody, who was happiest at home surrounded by her children.

In 1943 father was drafted into the German army at the age of 40, even after being deferred two times earlier due to arrhythmia. By this time, the army had lost so many men that they began drafting all men between the ages of 15 and 50 years who could walk. My father came home for the Christmas holidays that year prior to being sent to Marseille, France as part of the occupation forces there. My brother Fritz was born on August 21, 1944 in his absence.

Shortly after my father left, mom sat me down for a serious conversation. I was the oldest son and now "the man of the house". I realize, in retrospect, that I was a mere child of 9 years taking on this responsibility. Throughout the remainder of the war, I matured emotionally and intellectually at an accelerated pace due to a variety of unprecedented circumstances. These lessons would carry me throughout my entire life.

Father was captured by the American troops in late June of 1944 when they invaded southern France on the way north from Africa. We did not get news about him until after Christmas 1945. The German Department of War notified us that our father was missing in action and presumed to be a casualty of the battle around Marseille. My dear mother was sure that he was still alive and assured her children that we should not give up hope.[2] The Swiss Red Cross located him in a French POW camp on the island of Corsica in the Mediterranean Sea in late 1945. We had no communication with him during the 14 months he was there.

In father's absence, mother covered me with the invisible cloak of adulthood and we got along beautifully. In her wisdom, she nurtured me and fostered my independence and responsibility to the family. She taught me that my decisions were important and that I had to make them carefully: our family unit depended on it; we were a team.

My father didn't return home from the war and his imprisonment until just before Christmas 1946. He was in a fragile physical and emotional state. He had a very difficult time adjusting to life in a war ravaged country with four hungry and growing children and a very uncertain future. He was the head of a large household with a home only partially rebuilt. He lacked the money to buy the very scarce building materials needed to restore the house in a reasonable time span. The prospects for work and a good salary were also bleak. These factors combined took another toll on my father's personality. His constant bickering and negative attitude made him a difficult person to live with and he was not the father role model I envisioned now as a 12 year-old adolescent.

Father was certainly devastated when 3 year-old Fritz asked him, “When are you going back to the prisoner of war camp in France?” Young Fritz had never known our father and saw him as a disruptive intruder. I do not know if father resented the harmony built between my mother and the children during his absence, but it must have weighed on him. Today, I understand that he suffered from Post-Traumatic Stress Disorder (PTSD), which, at that time, was not recognized, let alone diagnosed.

We may have been poor, without a home and without much hope for the future, but mother always had a positive attitude and a comforting smile for each of us children. Our dear mother was a rock during that very difficult period of father’s adjustment and our uncertain livelihood. She kept everyone focused and happy, as much as possible, as we adapted to our new roles and responsibilities.

Since we lived in the country and we had the acreage to grow wheat, my mother ground the wheat for her bread and baked the loaves in a municipal baking oven. The oven was made out of sandstone. Her turn to bake was always between 5 and 7 p.m. on Tuesday night. I usually stopped by the community ***Backhaus*** (baking house) to help mother pull her cart loaded with freshly baked bread and ***Deie*** (Swabian pizza) home.

Deie was the dough and it was rolled out very thin. My mother topped it with cheese or sausage. Some families topped their Deie with sauerkraut. The Deie did not take much heat to bake. For that reason, it was always put in the oven before the large round loaves and was baked as the oven warmed up with the firewood. Everyone who used the community oven brought their own ingredients and firewood.

An interesting aspect of baking in the municipal facility is that no one wanted to be the first in line at the beginning of the daily 2-hour shifts. Since the ovens had cooled off from the previous day, the first person using the ovens in the morning had to use almost twice as much firewood as people baking later in the day. This was quite an issue. Not only was food scarce and rationed, but firewood was very expensive and hard to come by. Baking later in the day also took less baking time. This is the one time when the refugees, who came to Echterdingen during WWII, were indirectly penalized when given preferential treatment by being "first" in line.

When I was older and studying for my apprenticeship, I would bring Deie for lunch on Wednesday mornings. My "city" co-workers were quite willing to trade their pretzels for my pizza. Deie was as much a novelty to them as a pretzel was a welcome change for me.

For as far back in my childhood as I can remember, all food items were rationed.[3] Initially, the daily caloric allowance for a farmer or a person working in construction was 2400 calories. For women and all other occupations it was 1800 calories. For children up to adulthood it was 1200 calories. Newborn babies up to 2 years old and expectant or nursing mothers were the only people allowed whole milk. All others received skim milk. People received milk provided they had the ration coupons for this item. Ration cards were still purchased and people needed the money to buy them. The state regulated the cost and the prices were fixed.

Every person received a monthly ration card. As stated, the government regulated each person's caloric intake depending on age and profession. We quickly learned that ration cards were more precious than money. Our mother kept ours under lock and key. We also learned that having food coupons for certain items were no guarantee that the item was available in the store on the day we happened to go shopping. Coupled with the fact that there was no refrigeration, daily trips to the grocery and milk store as well as the butcher shop or the bakery were a necessity.[4]

My mother did most of the shopping during the week when my older sister, Marianne, and I were in school. On Saturdays, it was my job to go to the butcher shop to purchase our family's weekly ration of meat and sausage. The butcher shop opened at 7:00 a.m. and was usually sold out of various meat and sausage products just one hour later. The secret was to get there early if you didn't want to go home with an empty shopping basket.

I looked forward to Sundays because that was the only day of the week when my mother cooked a pork or beef roast (when it was available). Our family of 5 was entitled to 2 1⁄2 lbs. of meat each week (approximately 10 oz. per person).

When I went shopping, I wanted to be sure that I got first choice of whatever meat was available by being the first in line. That meant that I had to be at the butcher shop at least by 6:00 a.m. Since there were steps to the entrance, this also guaranteed a place to sit down during the wait by sitting on top of the pile of the daily newspapers when they were delivered. The newspapers made for a bit warmer seat, too.

I was in competition for arrival time with Frau Roth and the butcher was well aware of that. When I was first at the door, he would sometimes award me with a sausage end that was too small to sell, but a treat for me. When Frau Roth was first in line, she reminded him that she should also be given a treat. Herr Schaefer brushed her off by saying that she didn't look undernourished. "Besides," he said, "Eberhard is a growing boy." She responded by saying that she had a growing daughter at home. To which Herr Shaefer responded, "I don't see her standing in line."

As summer approached the sun rose earlier in the day and some of the regular Saturday morning customers started to come sooner to be first in line and sit on the steps. I continued getting up earlier and earlier each week to protect my spot on the butcher shop steps. I soon was up and at the butcher shop door by 5:00 a.m. to beat Frau Roth. If she beat me there, I would get up 15 minutes earlier the next week.

Usually by the time the store opened, there were at least 15-20 people waiting in line. Imagine all the town gossip I heard during the 1 1⁄2 hour wait. Many were aware of the competition between me and Frau Roth and they would each speculate as to who the first person would be the following Saturday.

Frau Roth hated to be second in line. She reminded me often that a boy my age should sleep in on Saturday mornings since we were at school by 7:00 a.m. each week day morning. Frau Roth even berated my mother one day while they met shopping. She told my mother that she should be ashamed of herself for making her son get up so early each Saturday morning to go shopping. My dear mother, hurt by the insinuation that she was a "bad mother," was embarrassed by the incident and cried while retelling the tale.

Frau Roth's actions had the opposite effect of her intention. My anger strengthened my resolve to stand my ground against her criticism and intimidation. I would not lose the waiting line battle with her. As the man of the house, I would not let my mother nor my siblings be deprived of meat. I stood in line initially during my mother's pregnancy. After Fritz was born, I continued to buy meat with Frau Roth's antics stimulating a mental game of wits to my self imposed sense of duty.

This life lesson taught me to fight for the important things in life and gave me resolve not to be like Frau Roth. I never begrudged her when she was first in line, accepting it in the spirit of competition. The situation helped me later to see other people's points of view in an argument that, to me, might seem ridiculous.

Friedrich & Erna Kehrer

Friedrich & Emma Bulach

Bulach Family 1943

Bulach Family 1980s

Echterdingen Gemeindehaus

Baking Bread and Holding Filderkraut

CHAPTER 2

GRADE SCHOOL MEMORIES

"Früh übt sich wer ein Meister werden will."
~ 'William Tell' von Friedrich Schiller

Early practice makes a master.

Schools suffered during the war. Teachers had to become members of Hitler's Nazi Party to qualify for a teaching position during the Third Reich. After the war, the educational system in Germany unraveled completely as all the teachers were dismissed to become "de-Nazified". This meant that all tenured teachers were jobless after V-E Day. The retraining and educating process took a long time and it was several years before the German educational system attained its pre-war standards at the elementary and university levels.

Most of the teacher replacements after the war were not qualified for their positions. In my case, we had a new male teacher, Herr Reschke, who was also a refugee. He spoke broken German. On one occasion he ordered one student to ***"Halt das Mund!"*** (Shut your mouth!) instead of ***"Halt den Mund!"*** He did not have our respect with his outburst or the grammatical error. Many of my classmates even considered him to be a communist agent.

School was always an adventure for me. I was inquisitive and never bored. The opportunity to learn and experience new things was a nice change from the chores at home. It was also something to which I could succeed. I never had much playtime with the neighborhood children because my mother had my time at home tightly programmed. Therefore, I considered school my playtime and I took full advantage of it. Learning came easily to me and my parents seldom had to encourage me to study. Grammar was my most difficult subject. Whenever our teacher, Herr Baier, quizzed the class on various subjects, he would turn to me if no one else could answer the question. He would say, "If anyone knows the answer, Eberhard surely does." He stroked my ego, challenging me to study even harder in my courses.

While on furlough from the army, my father visited our class. During recess he spoke to Herr Baier granting him permission to punish me if I didn't measure up to the teacher's expectations. Although I sat in the front row where the A students sat, I did not elude any spankings. Spankings were usually given to the troublemakers or poor students in the back of the room. My pride was hurt a few times when I became the scapegoat. However, to this day I admire Herr Baier. He was a strict disciplinarian and had complete order in his classroom of 55 students. He knew how to challenge his students to excel in their studies. He lost his temper occasionally, but was generally fair and willing to assist a student to understand the school material.

As a result of the war, paper and books were in short supply. The teacher put the daily lesson plan on the blackboard. Students would read the lesson plan until it was memorized. It was then erased and replaced by the next lesson. Once a week we also learned to sing a new folksong. Some songs had as many as 12 verses to memorize! We were graded on singing and penmanship.

I only recall one school fieldtrip in grades 6 and 7 to the ***Uhlberg Turm***. It is a lookout tower near the town of Hafner-Neuhausen, approximately 8 km from Echterdingen. We walked both ways since there were no school buses and no public transportation to that location. Later, we did have several mandatory "fieldtrips" during the war to the potato fields for ***Kartoffelkäfersuche*** (potato bug picking) and to the nearby airport for ***Granatsplittersammeln*** (shrapnel gathering).

The two school buildings in town were destroyed during the March 14, 1944 bombing that almost completely destroyed Echterdingen. Temporary facilities were devised for instruction in the Methodist Church, the Apostolic Church, the ***Turner Halle*** (gymnasium, community hall and movie theater), and an office building. However, these makeshift classrooms could only accommodate about half of the student population at any one time and the learning environment was quite poor.

There were six days of regularly scheduled school time Monday through Saturday. Each class and grade level received 5 days of instruction from 7:00 a.m. to 5:00 p.m.

with a one-hour break for lunch, which we had at home. Each class had one day off during the school week to alleviate the classroom space shortage. There were 6 weeks of summer vacation from mid-August through the end of September.

School sessions were often interrupted by air raids. We ran hurriedly down several flights of stairs into the ***Luftschutzkeller*** (air raid shelter) of a building's lowest level. If the classroom was in a municipal building that had no cellar, school children ran in all directions to nearby residences to seek shelter. Some times running home was not possible either because of distance or the vulnerability to strafing. We learned to cope with the situation and developed an immunity to fear as well as a false sense of invincibility.

Early one fall day in 1944, an American P-47 fighter plane strafed me as I was riding my bicycle on a blacktop road to our cabbage patch just outside of town. I was on my way to the garden to help my mother weed and hoe, quite aware of the aircraft by sight and sound. The plane peeled off from an 8-plane formation that patrolled the airspace around the Stuttgart airport, only 3 miles from Echterdingen. (The planes circled at an unusually low altitude to strafe any moving target. Perhaps it was entertainment for them, like target practice.) The plane accelerated its engine, putting me on notice that I had been spotted. I jumped off my bike and hit the ditch burying myself into the soft, smelly mud and covered my head with my arms trying to make myself invisible and stiff like a log. I could hear the aircraft cannons firing, the sparks flying and projectiles ricocheting off the pavement with a loud "ziii-ing". The projectiles also hit the soft ground around me with a thud sending dirt and dust everywhere.

I didn't dare leave the soggy ditch as my assailant took another sweep over me to see if I was moving. I lay perfectly still, holding my breath. Satisfied with his hit, the plane rejoined its formation. I hid for a short time until I was sure his squadron had headed back to France for refueling. When I finally felt safe, I got up and raised my fist to the sky screaming, "Some day I'll be one of you. I'll be the one shooting instead of being shot at!" (Thankfully, that never happened.)

The noise of the approaching airplane, the firing of its guns and the impact of the projectiles around me are forever etched in my memory. How I survived that horrible experience, I'll never know. I thank God that my guardian angel kept me alive.

My mother, working in a nearby field, also took cover between the cabbage rows to make sure she didn't become a target. As she saw me pedaling up the road, she gave a great cry of relief and hugged me tightly.

As soon as I turned 10 years old on April 24, 1944, I received a written notice to appear at a swearing in ceremony for the ***Hitler Jugend*** and the ***Jungvolk*** [5] at the local meeting hall. We children were eager to join this group because we were able to wear uniforms and play war games. It was just like American children who played cowboys and indians, firemen, policemen and "bad guys".

The Jungvolk assembled at least twice a week with meetings each Wednesday night at the assembly hall of the local brewery. We had orientation and classroom work. On weekends, depending on the time of year and the weather, we camped out in the nearby woods or in the meadows. We learned how to pitch a tent, start a campfire without matches and learned close order drills with different commands and marching formations. We were given air rifles to practice gun safety and marksmanship. Once we were familiar with the air rifles, we graduated to 22 caliber rifles.

The younger children watched with envy as the Hitler Jugend and the Jungvolk marched through town in their neat uniforms, singing and marching in precise step. It was quite a sight. Now that I was one of them, I enjoyed the discipline and the competition that we learned at those assemblies. The idea was that children with this type of training would have 8 years of Basic Training by the time they were 18 years old. The training and mental toughness that developed would provide the skills needed for military life and duty requiring little time for adjustment.

As I reflect on that time period, we had a lot of fun in spite of the military training. Given our predicament, we tried to make the best of every situation. We boys relished the thought of becoming grownups. It distracted us from war's reality in our midst: constant air raids, bombings, strafings, food shortages; lack of school buildings; complete nighttime blackouts.[6] We were never concerned with any nighttime criminal activity. Frankly, it never crossed our minds. People easily went out at night to visit family or friends. If it was a cloudy or rainy evening, the night skies would be quiet. No planes would be flying overhead.

In the Jungvolk we learned to respect our elders. If we were riding a train or a streetcar and someone older by 2 years or more and even 2 inches taller boarded, we would jump up and offer them our seat. We were taught to salute every person in uniform, whether policeman, fireman, soldier, mail carrier or street sweeper.

We took our training seriously. We were taught to go out of our way to help an elderly person cross the street or carry someone's shopping basket and just perform good deeds, just like American Boy Scouts. We were not permitted to smoke cigarettes until we turned 18 years old. We were permitted to drink alcoholic beverages, but we were not allowed to abuse the privilege.

Generally speaking, the Hitler Youth was a great organization. It kept children off the streets, kept them busy and kept them focused on worthwhile activities. Obviously, political brain washing was involved, but that is a different matter. For me, and the rest of my cohort, politics were left for the adults to manage. The benefits of our involvement were fun, a full stomach and staying alive during the air raids.

The stark reality of the war was that the uniforms we wore were the best item of clothing most of us children had. From a practical point of view, they were more readily available than any other kind of clothes. Clothing articles were rationed during the war just like everything else. Since our growing bodies changed from year to year, we were allowed to purchase a new uniform every two years, if they were available.

Those of us who lost our homes during the air raids had only the rags on our backs or possible hand me downs from others. I recall going to church on Christmas Eve and Easter wearing my uniform, as did many of the other children, because I had nothing else or nothing better to wear.

Going to church was not officially discouraged, but in the summer time we had overnight campouts from Saturday to Sunday. If a campout was not scheduled, we would assemble at the meeting hall or soccer field by 8:00 a.m. on Sundays. We seldom came home before 1:00 p.m. so that "conveniently" prevented us from attending church services.

One beautiful, hot summer afternoon in 1944, my neighbor and friend, Ernst Walker, and I went to the nearby Baggersee [7] to ride a float, which we had built out of scrap lumber and tree limbs. We were enjoying splashing each other with the cool, refreshing water when one of our other neighbor friends, Karl W., came by to remind us of the 6:00 p.m. assembly at the soccer field near the woods. Karl was one year older and the squad leader of our company of youth.

Ernst and I told him that we were having too much fun and that it was too hot to walk the two miles to the soccer field. About an hour later, our platoon leader, Kurt S. (3 years older than us), arrived on a bicycle with orders to follow him to the assembly – immediately! We weren't given time to go home to change into our uniforms or grab our bicycles. He required us to do "double time" all the way to the soccer field as he rode his bike behind us. When we slowed to an unacceptable pace, he would run into us with his bicycle wheel.

Once we arrived at the soccer field soaked in sweat, he ridiculed us in front of the entire assembly for going AWOL (absent without leave) and being out of uniform. If embarrassment was not enough, we were also assigned extra duties and tasks to perform as a reminder of our errant ways. This was an early taste and warning of military discipline.

Young girls had a similar organization called ***Bund Deutscher Mädel*** (Association of German Girls). They had similar meeting schedules, but instead of camping out and simulating war games, they were taught how to become homemakers. They were instructed in housekeeping, cooking, sewing, gardening, raising children and caring for handicapped individuals. They also wore uniforms. The girls wore skirts with hems below the knee, white blouses, and a neck scarf fastened in front with a leather knot. [8]

On many occasions, classes from our grade school assembled at the airport to search for and pick up shrapnel pieces from enemy bombs or German anti-aircraft artillery 88s that had fallen on the runway (***Granatsplittersammeln auf dem Rollfeld des Stuttgarter Flughafens***). This was done so that the German fighter planes, taking off and landing, would not get flat tires. We usually carried out this task on cloudy or rainy days when the planes, based at the airport, did not fly any missions. If weather prevented planes from flying, chances were great that enemy planes would not fly and therefore would not be a threat to the children on the tarmac either.

On one occasion, however, the weather cleared after a morning fog and the alarm sounded suddenly just as we fanned out over the far end of the runway to start our work. We were ordered to clear the runway quickly and take cover behind a huge earthen wall designed to protect German planes from any strafing aircraft.

As soon as we hugged the dirt and tall grass, eight Thunderbolts came swooping over the airfield two abreast at tree top level. Their targets were some parked and already damaged Me 109s at the end of the runway closest to the terminal. After that first pass, they must have concluded that they didn't damage the airplanes enough. All eight planes took a large loop and came back in formation for another attack. After the second pass, nothing resembling the airplanes was left. Their mission accomplished, the "Happy Eight" left us and we children were sent home running. We survived another scare, but wondered what would have happened to us had those P-47s come 15 minutes earlier when approximately 200 children were scattered around the area of the airplanes. We learned later that the most airworthy Me 109s were parked in a nearby forest where the "Happy Eight" could not spot them.

Prior to WWII, Germany did not have any potato bugs. In the late spring/early summer of 1943 when the fresh leaves of the new potato plants were blooming, American planes dropped potato bugs in small Kerr mason jars attached to small parachutes. Biological warfare! Millions of these bugs were dropped on the potato fields as a means of ruining the potato crop, thereby denying the German population its dietary staple. The potato bugs ate all the fresh leaves, thereby killing the young plant and reducing the potato harvest. This war tactic was meant to create hungry people, who would, in turn, have a lower morale and fighting spirit.

The jars were pint size and the parachutes were designed to land the jars slowly enough not to crush the bugs, but fast enough to crack the jar slightly when hitting the dirt or plants allowing the bugs to escape. The jars were wrapped in cellophane paper thin enough for the bugs to eat their way out of the jar if it did not break. We did find unbroken jars.

Entire classes, fourth grade and older, were required to go out into the fields early in the morning before the bugs began flying about. We checked the underside of the potato plants for the bugs and collected them in pails. After the search, we assembled in front of the City Hall and emptied the bugs into a pile, where they were doused with gasoline and set on fire.[9]

We only had to look for potato bugs for two months of each season in 1943, 1944 and 1945. After the war ended in 1945, no additional bugs were dropped. However, the bugs remained from earlier seasons. The whole exercise left a lasting impression on me because my hands turned yellow from handling the bugs and their excrement. It was a repugnant feeling, which I hated, but understood was part of life during the war years.

When I mention the potato bug incident to my American friends, no one is aware of this type of warfare. In fact, some people are incredulous and question my story. Some think I fabricated the entire scenario.

Eberhard dressed in Deutsches Jungvolk uniform.

Erné leading the Easter parade.

Men's group circa 1939. Friedrich Kehrer and Fritz Bulach sitting together in front row.

CHAPTER 3

WAR AND DEVASTATION

"Immer wenn du denkst es geht nicht mehr, kommt von irgendwo ein Lichtlein her, dass du es noch einmal wieder zwingst und von Sonnenschein und Freude singst. Leichter trägst des Tages Last und du wieder Kraft, Mut und Glauben hast!" ~ Maler Otto Löbke

Whenever you think that you can't go on, a little light comes from within propelling you forward, enabling you to sing of sunshine and happiness. The day's burdens are lightened and you have strength, courage and faith once again.

Since we lived only 2 km from the Stuttgart airport, we watched and listened to the German fighter planes take off and land. We soon learned to distinguish among the different types of German aircraft, the Messerschmitt Me 109 and Me 110, and the Focke-Wulf Fw 190 from the sound of their motors. We learned to distinguish the sounds of the American and British aircraft as well. As the end of the war drew near, the bombing and strafing became more frequent so these airplane identification lessons were reinforced daily. I call our education 'Airplane Identification 101'.

One of our pastimes was counting the German fighter planes taking off to intercept an incoming bomber formation that usually had no fewer than 200 4-engine bombers, either B-17s or B-24s. The British came with 4-engine Lancasters or twin engine Bristol Blenheims during all hours of the day or night. The daytime missions had at least 50 or more fighter escorts: Mustangs or Thunderbolts. Imagine how much damage the mere 30 Messerschmitts stationed at Stuttgart could do against those odds. We would always be curious to count the returning Me 109s, usually about 2 or 3 hours after take off, to see how many were missing. It was standard procedure for them to fly low over the airport before landing and tip their wings indicating they had a kill.

We children knew how many enemy planes were shot down and how many of ours failed to return well before the news media was informed. Sometimes we could hear a straggler come in late with a portion of a wing missing or smoking or even making a belly landing. We all noticed and reported, with great concern, that the number of Me 109s taking off to intercept Allied planes dwindled each day. Before long, all take offs ceased due to lack of fuel, lack of pilots and lack of air worthy airplanes.

Eight Allied Thunderbolts (P-47s) became daily fixtures controlling the sky over our area in the last months of the war. They circled the airport in order to shoot down any German airplane that might attempt a daytime takeoff or landing. The German aircraft were like sitting ducks. The anti-aircraft guns around the airport did not fire at the planes for fear of revealing their position.

The airplanes must have been close by in France because as soon as one set of eight planes left to refuel eight others would take their place. Fuel was certainly not an issue for them. These planes also dropped leaflets that said: ***"Wir sind die lustigen acht. Wir kommen bei Tag und bei Nacht."*** (We are the happy eight. We come by day and by night.)

On the night of March 14, 1944, air raid sirens over Echterdingen sounded again, just as they had many times before. My family and I huddled around the radio to hear how many bombers were coming and in which direction they were headed. We were on alert for a large British bomber force approaching the Stuttgart airspace. Everyone was instructed to go immediately to the air raid shelters.

Hurriedly, we gathered blankets and food as we headed to the fruit cellar. Mother stopped us and said, decisively, "Tonight we will go the neighbor's cellar across the street." The Walkers' house was older and bigger than our house and its cellar was larger and deeper and had thicker walls. Since mother was three months pregnant, she felt more secure with Herr Walker in the house, too.

As we crossed the street, we could see flares on parachutes being dropped by a few scout planes. They illuminated the night sky to direct the bomber units to the nearby airport target. Shrapnel from thousands of anti-aircraft gun shells that exploded flack ammunition into the air were already whistling all around us. The debris landed like heavy hail or gravel on the clay tile roofs of houses and other buildings nearby. The motors of hundreds of approaching airplanes sounded like a fast approaching tornado; a sound forever engraved in my memory. A strong wind carried the parachute flares away from the airport and headed directly toward our town. This caused us deep concern.

Herr Walker was not drafted into the military because of a deformed foot that made him unable to march long distances. Also, the fact that he raised vegetables and fruit, that could feed our community, also spared him conscription even toward the end of the war. The harsh reality of the war years was that a handicap such as his would deem him an undependable soldier and his expertise was sorely needed on the "home front".

Herr Walker made sure that all members of his own family, those of his tenant family of three and the four of us (mother, 2 sisters and me) were safely inside the cellar before securing the metal fire door. He was concerned that Echterdingen would bear the brunt of the bombing due to the wayward flares. "They certainly won't take those bombs back to England," he shouted as we heard the first bombs exploding in the distance.

The ground vibrated slightly as the noise of the exploding bombs and artillery shells came closer and became more intense. Our initial feeling of security provided by the thick stone cellar walls began to dissipate. The closer the bombs were, the more earthquake-like vibrations we felt and the cellar door rattled. We huddled closer together.

Suddenly there were several ear shattering explosions in close succession just outside the Walker home that caused the lights to flicker. Complete and sudden darkness followed. Some of the children began to cry. Frau Walker started to recite the Lord's Prayer. We all were expecting death and a direct hit with the next explosion. Miraculously we were spared.

Fräulein Storz, the spinster daughter of the couple renting portions of the Walkers' second floor, became almost hysterical. She was 35 years old and somewhat mentally handicapped as it was. Every time that a bomb exploded in close proximity to us, she passed gas uncontrollably. I was huddled directly behind her wondering when she would "run out of gas." Even in this most frightful situation, my 10 year old mind was easily distracted by that odd sound.

In the meantime, Herr Walker lit some candles he had stored in the cellar for an emergency such as this. In the candlelight, we could see that everyone was covered in fine white dust that had fallen from the mortar joints of the ceiling above us. We looked as if we had been working in the bakery and were covered by flour. One by one we started coughing and sneezing. The women quickly moistened handkerchiefs and towels with some of the drinking water we had with us. We held them over our noses to prevent inhaling the gritty dust.

The explosions became less frequent and more distant. Soon there were no more airplane noises, no more vibrations and no more falling dust. The familiar explosions of the German anti-aircraft artillery (the famous “88”) became fewer and more distant as well. As they tried to shoot down some of the last enemy bombers that were also relieving their loads and returning home. The planes retreated empty.

We checked each other for injuries. Fräulein Storz fainted. She came to as her father washed her face with cold water and gave her a shot of Schnapps to drink. We children were even given some of the brandy to wash down the dust collected in our mouths and throats. Herr Walker unlatched the heavy cellar door to go outside and see if it was safe to exit our cool, damp shelter. The “all clear” siren did not sound because the electrical service had been wiped out by the heavy bombing. Ernst, Fritz Walker’s oldest son, who was 1 1⁄2 years older than me, begged his father to allow him and me to come up with him. Although the explosions lasted only 30 minutes, it seemed like an eternity and Herr Walker feared the worst. We wanted to see the extent of the damage. Herr Walker agreed to let us follow him before the other adults. We were not prepared for what we saw. The sight took our breath away.

My first impulse was to look toward my house. The roof and the second floor were engulfed in flames. Mother, Marianne and I ran quickly to see if we could salvage any of our furniture and belongings from the first floor before the flames consumed the entire house. Herr Walker was at our heels and forbid us from entering the house. He went in himself and handed some of the small furniture through our living room windows before it became too dangerous for him. He feared that the second floor would collapse onto the first floor at any moment.

Shortly thereafter Herr Storz came running to tell us that two small fires, caused by flying sparks, had started the Walkers' roof on fire. Quickly we assisted the two men putting ladders to the roof and formed a bucket brigade passing up water from the rain barrel to the men. They dampened burlap sacks to douse the flames before they could spread and cause any serious damage. We kept vigil over the roof the entire night and through the morning to be sure flying sparks and shifting winds did not reignite the roof. This house was one of the few remaining in our neighborhood.

The smoke-filled air burned our eyes. Although it was a cold mid-March night, we were hot from the many fires around us. The adrenalin rush from all the excitement kept us awake, too. Our house had been hit by both a concussion bomb and a fire bomb. The concussion bomb had penetrated the roof and the second and first stories. The fire bomb had set on fire all the exposed timber of the roof structure eventually consuming the entire structure down to the basement walls and ceiling, which were made of concrete and stone.

Although it was close to midnight, the fiery inferno caused an eerie daylight glow. Huge billows of smoke were propelled skyward by the rush of oxygenated air needed to feed hundreds of fires consuming homes, barns and public buildings as far as the eye could see. It seemed as if the sky was burning. Combine several of today's large municipal firework displays firing at once and you might be able to imagine the sight before us.

Concussion bombs caused the initial destruction tearing buildings apart much like that of a tornado. These bombs were followed by phosphorous and fire bombs that ignited the exposed combustible materials – timber, furniture, hay, animals. Because bombs had destroyed the waterlines, fires burned unchecked for several hours. Some ruins continued to smolder for days. The stench of burnt wood, other building materials, organic matter and burnt animal flesh from cows, horses and other farm animals filled the air for weeks.

Later in the night, volunteer firefighters from surrounding communities and soldiers from the nearby airport came to help salvage whatever possible. Even Russian prisoners of war held at the airport were ordered to assist and search for survivors buried in their cellars. They also had to round up livestock that had been spooked by the explosives and scattered to the countryside.

In the morning, we surveyed the remains of Uhlandstrasse 13. All that was left of our home was a huge pile of blackened bricks and cinder blocks, broken roof tiles and smoldering remnants of wooden beams and wall partitions. It was a home built only 13 years earlier by my parents, who had saved by living frugally.

This air-raid experience dampens my desire to watch firework displays on July 4th and New Year's Eve. The night of the bombing was the ultimate firework display created by humankind, but with deadly consequences. Perhaps the Great Chicago Fire of 1871 or the Hinckley, Minnesota Forest Fire of 1894 might compare equally.

That night turned our lives upside down. Our town was almost wiped off the map by the British Air Force. We had no time to feel sorry for ourselves as we had much to accomplish. We had to find a place to live and start cleaning up the rubble from our destroyed house to salvage as much as possible. There was no government agency to come in and assist in the clean up, nor was there aid for reconstruction. Every person and household had to fend for themselves. We stayed with the Walkers for another day with only the clothes on our back. Then Frau Loehrl, another neighbor, invited us to move into her apartment with her and her two sons. Her husband was away in the army.

In later years, I asked my mother what made her decide that we should go to the Walkers the night of the bombing. She answered simply, that she had no reason except for a premonition that it was the right thing to do. She also felt safer with a man nearby. Her intuition saved our lives.

After the war, we also learned that 863 British 4-engine Lancaster bombers, the largest bomber force assembled at that time, intended to strike the Mercedes Benz and Bosch industrial complexes to the north in Stuttgart. However, due to cloud cover and fog, spotter planes were unable to locate their intended target. The bombers dropped their deadly loads 8-10 miles too early nearly destroying 10 farm communities and came close to hitting the nearby airport.[10]

My family moved into the 3-story house of Alice and Elsbeth Engel, two spinster sisters. They lived about one block away from our demolished house. The Engels lived on the third floor under the roof and rented out the lower two stories. We lived there 3 1⁄2 years until we could move in to our own rebuilt home.

Max and Käthe Goller and their two children, Edeltraut and Heini (Heinrich) lived on the first floor. The Gollers took in thc Metzger family whose home, closer to the center of town, was also destroyed. The Metzger family consisted of Wilhelm and Nanele, their son Eberhard (15 years old, my sister Marianne's age), their daughter Annerose (10 years old, my age) and Fritz, Wilhelm's father, a retired plumber. The two eldest Metzger sons, Paul and Ernst, were serving in the German army. Eberhard Metzger was drafted into the Hitler Youth artillery crews that manned the "88" anti-aircraft batteries.

Frau Loehrl rented the second floor apartment with her two boys and invited us to move in with her. One month after we moved in, she and her family moved back to her hometown in the ***Schwarzwald*** (Black Forest region). The Spannenberger family consisting of Dr. Spannenberger, his wife, Antoinette, their daughters, Sylvia and Sybille, and son, Helmi took over the Loehrls' rented space. The second floor had a kitchen, a family room, two bedrooms, a screened in balcony and one bathroom with a stool and a bathtub with cold running water. My mother and I and my two sisters rented the smaller bedroom of the apartment. The kitchen, living room, bathroom and balcony were shared. A small room in the cellar was used for storing potatoes, vegetables, apple cider and wine.

Frau Spannenberger was a French aristocrat and it didn't take us long to realize that she disliked sharing living space. Dr. Spannenberger, a dentist, was a kind and understanding gentleman and his wife was sweet when he was home, but quite sour when he was gone to tend to the wounded at the Stuttgart hospital as part of his National Guard assignment. I remember my mother crying often at the humiliation and indignation we endured at the hands of Frau Spannenberger. My mother's pain was compounded by the news that our father was with the German Occupation Forces in France and later reported missing in action. The fact that we were without a "head of household" further diminished our status to "homeless" and increased Frau Spannenberger's insufferable and arrogant demeanor toward us. I didn't understand the full impact and source of our suffering until many years later.

Since five different families lived in the Engels' house, cleaning the stairway from top to bottom rotated weekly by family. The job included sweeping and shoveling snow from all the sidewalks around the house and the main sidewalk leading to the street and the street gutter in front of the property. This was my job when it became our turn.

Even during the final phase of the war, air raids were frequent and continued almost daily. Rushing to the cellar became routine. The Engels' house had an old, deep cellar and it was my job to carry Sybille Spannenberger down there. She was about 1 year old. I grabbed the wicker basket where she slept and ran while Frau Spannenberger carried Sylvia who was about 3 years old. Marianne or my mother carried my brother Fritz who was 6 months old.

In spite of the gravity of the situation, we children tried to make a game of it by seeing who could get to the cellar the fastest and carry the most things. Picking the best spot on the bench or apple crate for sleeping was the reward for getting there first. It's amazing that I never dropped Sybille.

We were frequently confined to the cellar for several hours before the "all clear" siren sounded. We children became restless, hungry and thirsty. Since food was scarce, we learned to share whatever was available. Our stomachs were seldom full, but we had plenty to drink in the way of apple cider, mineral water and beer. I don't recall ever being thirsty. There were actually times when I looked forward to the next long alarm because our mothers somehow produced a piece of candy or chocolate to temper our rambunctious behavior and complaining.

During the summer and fall seasons when the berries, apples, pears, cherries and plums ripened we could eat all the homegrown fruits we wanted. I recall climbing a plum tree before going to school to eat two handfuls of plums for breakfast. That, incidentally, would be my dinner after school as well.

It took about a week for the fires to burn themselves out after the bombing of Echterdingen. Lack of water pressure and the need of humans and livestock to have whatever precious water was available took precedence over dousing burning buildings. Assessing the total damage and the cleanup of the aftermath started as soon as the fires died.

My mother reiterated what she had told me earlier, "Eberhard, you are the man of the house and it is your responsibility to clean up and salvage as many building materials as you are able for rebuilding purposes. You will have to do this in your spare time." She had enough to do with the household chores, working in the vegetable garden and caring for us children.

Whenever I didn't attend school, I was over at the house ruins cleaning mortar off the bricks with a brick hammer or hatchet in order to reuse them. The lime and cement contained in the old mortar were very tough on my hands. They ate away at the skin. Since I was young and had no calluses on my hands, the job proved to be very painful.

Gloves and Band-Aids would have helped a great deal. However, these were luxury items and simply not available. Returning to school was a welcome reprieve that allowed my hands to heal and relieved the pain in my back and right arm.

I picked up all the loose brick, roof tile, boards and beams that I could carry. It wasn't long before it became evident that I needed someone stronger to tear apart some of the heavy partitioned walls and the remaining beams from the roof.

My mother learned from the mayor's office that there were Russian prisoners of war at the airport who were fixing and maintaining the runways after the bombings. They were available on a daily basis to help with cleanup in town when they were not busy repairing runways. The only requirement was signing them out of the camp and feeding them.

My mother dispatched me to the airport to get some Russian prisoners to assist me with the cleanup and salvage. The guards laughed at me when I came and pleaded my case for the Russian POW They would not sign out a prisoner to a child. I returned crushed and downhearted.

Mother spoke to her brother, Ludwig Hertfelder, my godfather. He was captain of the volunteer fire department and spoke to the mayor about our situation. The mayor, in return, wrote a letter instructing the prison guards to find two of the most trustworthy men among the prisoners and send them home with me. The guards selected two older Russian men and told them to go with me and do whatever I needed done. Furthermore, they were never to leave my sight as I had written authorization over them. If they were ever caught without German accompaniment, they would be shot on the spot. People teased me by asking, "Where are your Russian body guards today?"

I was relieved to finally have help with my salvaging task, but in my 10-year old innocence, I had no understanding of the depth of responsibility I had for the lives of these two men. When we worked together, the men shadowed me wherever I went. One day I wandered off to the bathroom without thinking that I had left the men alone. When I returned, the men stared at me hard without saying a word. I realized how much we depended on each other for one another's survival. Although we could not communicate verbally, we seemed to communicate at a higher, more intuitive level via looks and gestures, which worked well over time.

The two Russian men, Ivan and Peter, were a great help and they enjoyed being away from the prison camp. They came in the spring and summer during the daytime. Although we had very little food ourselves, they were fed better with us due to mother's vegetables and the berries and fruit trees in our yard. Our yard was a good size by German standards and my father had planted a variety of fruit trees and berry bushes so that in the summer the yard looked like "a jungle" according to my mother.

We had a dozen or so chickens that enabled us to have eggs as well. Ivan and Peter grinned from ear to ear when mother gave them an occasional hardboiled egg. They were allowed to eat as much fruit as they wished. That was certainly not available in the camp. Mother was grateful for their work and showed them compassion by washing and mending their jackets and shirts on the hot days when they worked bare-chested.

Because Ivan and Peter went wherever I went, they took advantage of using the indoor bathroom when I went inside. Frau Spannenberger's obvious displeasure was not lost on us. Therefore, we decided to build an outhouse in the yard with the scrap lumber. This saved us a trip and Frau Spannenberger's cross look.

Occasionally, Ivan and Peter took scrap pieces of wood back to the camp with them. The wood was charred on the outside and I thought they would use them for firewood. One day when I went to get them, they both had an large bulge in their jacket pocket. They had to show the guard what they had, but motioned to him that he shouldn't let me see what they had. Once we had arrived at my yard, they each pulled out a carved tank. One tank was a Russian T-34, the other tank was a German Tiger. Each was carved to scale with turning turrets and markings burned into the wood with small nails they must have heated up over a fire.

They watched me carefully as I accepted the gifts. What an unexpected treat! I was overjoyed. I looked to them thanking them over and over again. I noticed Ivan's eyes welling up with tears. Surely he was thinking about his own son who was about my age and wishing he could have made such a toy for him, too. (He had shown me a picture of his wife and son earlier.) The tanks were so realistic and each of my friends also wanted one.

By the end of the 1944 summer, we had everything pretty well salvaged and cleaned up to the foundation walls that were still standing and reusable. We stacked bricks, roof tiles, boards and timber. We sawed off all the burnt portions of the oak timbers that could be reused and the rest we left for firewood.

Since the foundation was almost intact and the basement and cellar portions of the house were still standing, with the exception of a few holes in the floor or ceiling where the bombs hit, we covered the entire area with waterproof materials to keep the water out of the basement. Nevertheless, there were still times when I had to bail out water from the basement and cellar after a rainfall. But there was at least a place where we could store our potatoes, apples, pears and other fruits and berries harvested from our garden. My mother canned a good amount of fruit in Weck canning jars.

Bombings and strafing at the airport by the Allied Powers intensified again at the end of the summer. Because of that, Ivan and Peter were no longer allowed to come to our home to work. I often wonder what happened to these kind men and how, and if, they survived the war.

At the start of the war, farmers and male hired hands were immune from the draft. They were needed at home to work the land that produced the food for the German population. However, as the German fronts expanded and casualties increased, these men were also called up to service and their positions at home were replaced with male prisoners of war.

I remember approximately 20 French prisoners of war assigned to farmhouses in our area where the husband had been drafted into the German army or was a war casualty. These men lived with the family taking on the role as "the man of the house." They were to assume the hard labor of the absent men. They wore the French soldier's uniform and on the back of their jackets or shirts they wore a large white KG insignia for ***Kriegsgefangener*** (POW).[11] The German army could not spare soldiers to guard prisoners so they hoisted the responsibility on families. To my knowledge there was never an incident where a prisoner escaped or harmed any family member. There was a mutual understanding between the POW and the family. The POW provided sorely needed physical labor in exchange for shelter, food and security.

In addition to the French prisoners, there were also several Polish prisoners of war assigned to farmers or to the local Sauerkraut cannery. The Polish were actually the first POWs brought to our region as early as 1939 when the German army marched into Poland on September 1, 1939 and took occupation in the course of 18 days. After 5 years in Germany, these men could speak German quite well and felt at home in their forced surroundings.

They all returned home after they were liberated in 1945. However, three men, Stan, Josef and Johann returned to Echterdingen. Stan worked in an office. Johann and Josef remained bachelors. Josef even inherited some land when his former employer died. Life in Germany, even after losing the war, had more to offer them than life in a liberated and victorious Poland.

Jean Bézy, a Frenchman, stayed on with his farm family to protect them from any harm that might come due to the French military occupying our portion of Germany in the early days of the Armistice. In fact, as the French tanks set up outside our town to shell us prior to marching in, Jean interceded on the town's behalf by convincing the commander that there were no German army defenders left in the town. By his actions, Jean saved many lives. Later, he returned to France to visit his family and returned a week later to marry the German farmer's daughter where he had lived. He became a German citizen and was a well-respected member of the community.

Civilians and POWs alike believed the war would end with the Allies victorious. These were times of great distress and hopelessness. Our minds concentrated on our basic needs, survival and our next meal. Regardless of social status, civilian or prisoner, our predicament was the same. We were all victims. Bombs did not distinguish between friend and foe. Pilots in the Mustang or Thunderbolt cockpits could not differentiate civilian, military and POW personnel when strafing the countryside. Although the euphemistic term "collateral damage" did not enter the English language until recently, we lived in fear of becoming a statistic of such a term. We all shared the fear of either being killed in an air raid or starving to death before liberation occurred. This common thread bound people together. We literally "lived one day at a time." Every sunrise and every food morsel was precious and gave us one more day beyond destruction. The people of Echterdingen longed for freedom from the yoke of a fanatic, self-destructive dictatorship. For POWs the end of war meant a return to their families. The thought of returning home was what kept these men alive.

Additional wars and research have shown time and time again that returning home is difficult. Shock and depression and inability to re-adapt have been documented. However, in dismal situations 'home' is the thought that spurs a person on, providing the willpower to exist.

The French Colonial Troops that liberated us in Echterdingen were colonial troops from Morocco, Tunisia, Algeria and other parts of northern Africa. Most of the men were stationed at the nearby airport, yet some occupied the portion of the town hall still standing. Tents were also set up as one artillery battery at the train station. The enlisted men stayed in tents while the officers confiscated houses that didn't get damaged and set the homeowners out on the street.

These troops did not make a good impression. The men were unshaven, their uniforms were dirty and smelly, and the men reeked of garlic, sweat and alcohol. Women feared them due to rumors of rape and pillage by these troops. Farmers lost poultry and eggs to the troops as well.

As losers in this war, we soon realized that, as Germans, we had no rights or privileges. 'To the victor belong the spoils." Property, food, material goods and human dignity were all taken at will. I learned this first hand.

I was walking down ***Stuttgarter Strasse*** (Stuttgart Street) on an errand when a jeep with a French colonial soldier pulled up and asked me for directions to the airport in broken German. I told him. Then he pulled out a candy bar and asked me to hop in the jeep to show him the way. The jeep ride and candy were extremely enticing for a young boy. I jumped in and soon realized that I had made a grave mistake. He drove to an apple orchard instead of the airport.

His friendly, smiling face disappeared. This man jumped me and held me down with a 12" bowie knife to my throat for submission as he assaulted me. His eyes were wild like a raging bull. When he was satisfied, he threatened to slit my throat with his knife if I ratted on him. He then took off and left me behind.

Here I was, 11 years old, bewildered by what just happened. This aspect of war showed me more evil in the world. I didn't understand what had just happened and I didn't know how I would explain the blood on my underwear to my mother. She didn't believe me when I told her that I was injured while climbing trees. I confessed and my mother wept bitterly.

The following day mother took me to the doctor. The nurse bandaged me and told my mother to report it to the French town commander at the courthouse. We had to wait several hours to be seen by the French officer. When my mother related the problem via the interpreter, the officer laughed and returned to his office saying, "How dare you take up my valuable time with such a small problem? You German pigs should be grateful the soldier didn't kill him." We were both crushed by this additional cruelty.

As time progressed, I was able to put the incident aside; a child's strong defense mechanism at work. It was harder for my mother to do so. Reflecting on the time period post-war and pre-peace, there were untold numbers of traumatic events that made us all immune to shock and disappointment. Everyone was at the mercy of the French forces occupying our town. Just when conditions seemed to reach their worst, the French colonials were replaced by the American troops in June. Conditions improved, but food was still quite scarce and rationing remained part of life.

I am not bitter, nor do I hate the French. Some of the German troops had equally appalling behavior when occupying foreign lands, too. I learned to distinguish between good and evil in humans. I also have learned to deal with adversity rather than lament it.

May 8, 1945, V-E Day (Victory in Europe) was the day when war ravaged Europe finally stopped bleeding. Mercifully, the senseless, yet unavoidable killing finally came to a long hoped for end. It cost about 40 million lives in the European theater and brought an end to the daily air raids and the fear of not living to see another day.

While the victorious Allied Forces were jubilant (and rightfully so) because they destroyed "Hitler's Evil Empire", it did not mean that the suffering of the civilian population in Germany and other war ravaged countries came to a sudden end. Yes, there were no more bombs, but there were no jobs, no money, no hope and there was the daunting task of cleaning up the mountains of rubble that were once cities, towns and factories. The dead needed burying and the long bread lines and empty shelves in grocery stores continued for a seemingly endless period of time. Rationing of food, clothing, lumber and other building materials continued for three more years until 1948 when the new Deutsche Mark (DM) currency was introduced to replace the old Reichsmark.

We were at the mercy of a military government that was more interested in hunting down ex-Nazi war criminals than feeding the undernourished population, which also suffered from a serious housing shortage. The housing shortage became more pronounced with the influx of returning German army veterans from POW camps. More important, the housing shortage was further exacerbated by millions of refugees who, because of their German heritage, were fleeing persecution and certain death from the advancing Russian armies. These ethnic Germans had been invited, several generations ago to come and teach the people of Russia, the Balkan countries and the Baltic States about agriculture, forestry, technology, construction and education. These governments provided the German immigrants with homesteads wherever they settled.

Because of the Allied bombing raids, between 40-80% of all German city dwellings were destroyed or uninhabitable. More than half of the country's infrastructure was destroyed or in dire need of maintenance or replacement. Stuttgart's own streetcar and railroad system was in disrepair. At least 50% of all major autobahn and railroad bridges were destroyed, if not by the Allies, then by the desperate retreat of the German army itself.

The town of Echterdingen (pop 3,000) was directed by the American military government to receive 40 refugee families from the East, approximately 200 people. Where would they live? Where would the children go to school? Our own townspeople were without proper shelter and our school system was broken down.

Like most communities in our geographical location, Echterdingen was 95% Protestant prior to WWII. The majority of townspeople attended the Evangelical Church, which was prominently located in the center of town next to the courthouse and the town square. This was the church in which my mother was baptized, confirmed and married. My siblings and I, and Erné as well, were also baptized and confirmed in this church. Three other smaller churches were scattered in other neighborhoods: a Methodist church, a New Apostolic church, the ***Hahnsche Gemeinde*** (a meeting hall for Protestant prayer groups). These were the three buildings used as substitute classrooms for several years until the two school buildings were rebuilt.

Most of the refugees coming to Echterdingen were Catholic. Funds and materials were unavailable for building a separate Catholic church so they were granted specific worship times in the Evangelical Church. The newcomers were gradually integrated into the community, but not without some conflict in the beginning. The saying "misery loves company" comes to my mind and the Bible verse 1 Corinthians 12:26: "And if one member suffers, all the members suffer with it; if one member is honored, all the members rejoice with it."

The newly formed and temporary puppet government controlled by the occupation forces awarded a set amount of money to each refugee for relocation expenses. This upset our own citizens who had lost their homes and also their livelihoods and jobs due to the bombings, yet there was no monetary compensation for them. The government representatives tried to placate us by saying, "At least you did not have to flee your homeland." Naturally, this did not sit well with our own homeless, my mother included. Such a policy created ill feelings between the old and new citizenry.

Slowly, for most of us, the quality of life improved. More food and building materials became available, but they were still rationed. The black market in Germany thrived because the Reichsmark became more and more worthless with each passing day due to inflation. There was severe unemployment and there were hundreds of applicants for every job opening as the bombed out factories and office buildings were rebuilt and began operating.

I was also caught up in the job search while looking for an apprenticeship position. Though my academic test scores qualified me for high school and college, my parents did not have the financial resources to send me. Our house needed to be rebuilt and my father had just returned from the prisoner of war camp.

Adolf Dreher, a man who served in the German army with my father, was employed at the Keese Mfg. Co. as a lathe operator after he returned home from the war. That factory, located in Ostheim, a suburb of Stuttgart, was partially bombed out as well. The damaged portion of the factory was being rebuilt as well as the damaged metal cutting machines so desperately needed for the manufacturing of printing presses, which was their product. After several job interviews, I was fortunate to receive a position as a machine builder's apprentice (similar to a tool & die maker). My test scores and Herr Dreher's reference stood out and I was fortunate to be selected out of at least a dozen applicants. I was 14 1⁄2 years old when I started this job in September 1948.

I am extremely proud of my German homeland and the progress that was made in rebuilding the entire country after WWII. Following Erné's and my annual visit to Germany in 2011, I wrote down several observations and impressions.

At that time, Germany out-performed the United States both politically and economically. The coalition government of CSU (***Christliche Socialistische Union***) and FDP (***Freie Demokratische Partei***)[12] found consensus or a plan of action when confronted with difficult tasks.

Germany's highly skilled and motivated labor force was also among the highest paid in the industrial world, yet their products remained competitive in cost while maintaining high quality and performance standards. Also, many of the major industrial companies such as Mercedes Benz, Bosch, Beyer, BMW, Siemens, Audi and Stihl had non-voting union representation on their Board of Directors. The employer-employee relationship was based on cooperation and mutual respect versus the more confrontational and often anti-progress and anti-business sentiments found in the United States.

In 2011, I found Germany to be one of the cleanest countries in the world based upon my many travels. The public transportation system was among the most efficient and maintained systems that I have ridden. And, it was always punctual. The German unemployment rate was also 5.7% versus the United States unemployment rate of 9.1%.[13]

I always enjoyed driving on the Autobahn and think that it would be worthwhile for Minnesota drivers to learn the discipline and courtesy of the Autobahn roadways. I liked the thrill of driving at 180 km/hour, but had to remember to stay out of the passing lane if I didn't want to push up to 200 km/hour speeds. Semi-trucks maintained a 100 km/hour speed limit with passing in the middle lane only. And, a most impressive driving rule was the restriction of semi-truck traffic on the Autobahn from noon Saturdays until midnight Sundays.

I liked the fact that German utilities are buried underground instead of being hung on poles like in the US. Above ground utilities can subject communities to power outages when power lines go down during a storm. Germany was also on the leading edge of alternate energy production in the areas of solar and wind.

In the hospitality and dining industry, I was truly impressed by the use of real glass and ceramic serving dishes instead of paper and plastic. The annual sauerkraut festival in our hometown of Echterdingen has seen attendance as high as 40,000 people. At any time during that event, I have never seen any broken bottles or dishes at the side of the road and the only paper used were the napkins.

At the end of WWII, the German people were quite eager to take on the American way of life and were receptive to democracy and capitalism. This served them well and the rebuilt country prospered. Perhaps now in the year 2020, we Americans should return to the original values and advice that we so freely gave to the world and follow them ourselves.

Many older Americans alive today (often referred to as "the Greatest Generation") are aware of the Marshall Plan that provided loans for all of the war-torn countries of World War II. The purpose of the Marshall Plan was to help these countries rebuild their factories and infrastructures as soon as hostilities ceased. It provided jobs for the people, put food on their tables and, most importantly, jumpstarted the economies. Not to be overlooked was the idea of providing hope for a better future under a representative form of government.

Germany probably received the largest amount of money under the Marshall Plan. Major cities were severely destroyed, a consequence of the urban location of industrial plants dedicated to the war effort. The Allies did a very good job of wiping out these industrial plants. Germany, to its credit, made good and instant use of the financial support by becoming (within a short 15 years after the war's end in 1945) the famous ***Wirtschaftswunder*** (economic miracle). In fact, Germany became the third strongest world economy in GDP (gross domestic product) by 1965 behind the US and the Soviet Union.[14] It remained in that position until Japan outperformed the country for after 1975. Since the 1991 demise of the Soviet Union and the 2012 slump of the Japanese economy, Germany maintains the strongest European economy. And, is second in the world exports only to the United States using statistics from the late 1990s. The generosity and munificence of the Marshall Plan has been given its well-deserved and bountiful kudos in other pieces of literature.

There was, however, another equally important humanitarian plan that benefited Europe. I call it the Hoover Plan. It is a food relief program devised by former President Hoover[15] to feed the severely undernourished school children in war-torn Europe. He probably saved my life along with hundreds of thousands of other starving children. Herbert Hoover was a member of the Quaker faith and toured war-ravaged Europe in 1947. After seeing the great need for food, Hoover discussed the emergency with his friend, President Harry S. Truman. He received permission to empty the Quaker Oats warehouses to begin providing supplemental meals to Europe on April 14. The amount of food donated totaled 40,000 tons.

At this point, every school aged child between the age of 6 and 14 years in Germany was fed one healthy portion of Quaker Oats daily. The oatmeal or ***Hooverspeisung*** (Hoover meals) was cooked in large booyah kettles, remnants of the German army field kitchens. We didn't care what the food was cooked in as long as we could fill our stomachs during the five school days each week. We were happy, Samuel Johnson's English dictionary definition of oats notwithstanding. OATS: a grain, which in England is generally given to horses, but in Scotland supports the people.[16] Yet, like normal children, it wasn't long before we nicknamed the oatmeal ***Elefantenrotz*** or elephant snot. The color and texture was never too appetizing, but it did put meat on our bones.

Several years ago our family toured the Herbert Hoover Library in West Branch, Iowa where Hoover was born. On display were many letters of gratitude from German, Dutch, Belgian and French children who owed their lives to this kind-hearted and generous individual.

Ask a European living during that era and they will certainly acknowledge what Herbert Hoover did for them. In my opinion, Herbert Hoover was one of the world's greatest humanitarians of the 20th century. He can certainly be listed among other great humanitarians: Mahatma Gandhi, Martin Luther King, Albert Schweitzer, Mother Theresa, to name only a few.

Because of the scarcity of food by the end of WWII and then post-WWII, many children my age suffered from various health conditions as a result of poor nutrition and lack of vitamins necessary for proper growth. Our bodies were susceptible to tuberculosis, boils and dental disease. In my case, an open sore developed below my right knee that would not respond to treatment. Dr. Fritz Huber told me that my body's lack of resistance to infection was due to the lack of necessary vitamins in my diet.

Dr. Huber tried several different salves and medications, but nothing seemed to heal the sore. The sore grew deeper advancing to my shinbone while also oozing blood and puss. One day he cautioned me that if we saw no improvement soon, he would have no choice but to amputate my right leg below the knee. There was a medicine in powdered form that could dry up the wound and begin the healing process, but it was not available in Germany. We mailed the doctor's prescription to Uncle Gene Bulach, my father's brother, in the United States. He promptly brought the prescription to his physician, who filled it. Uncle Gene then mailed the medicine to us in Germany.

The infection slowed immediately after the first application of this powder. With continued treatments the wound gradually dried up and the excruciating pain subsided. This took a good 4 months and left me with a large scar 5" below my right knee as a reminder of that time period when I was 13 years old.

An incident concerning health and school that I remember, I record here. This teacher, to his credit, was one our schools best teachers and I liked and respected him until we had this unpleasant episode

One day I came to school late because I had to stop at the health clinic to have Dr. Huber treat and re-bandage my wound. Our teacher, Herr Schauer, reprimanded me for being late. After telling him my problem and showing him my bandaged leg, he directed me to open the bandage to convince him that I was telling the truth. He almost fainted and apologized after seeing the bloody mess thereby instructing me to recover the wound. I was furious and distraught over the fact that he would not believe me, especially since I had been seeing the doctor for months on a weekly basis on my way to school. I ran out of the class, back to the doctor's office in order to have the wound re-dressed. Dr. Huber, who was never at a loss for words, said, "***Was ist den der Schauer für ein Arschloch, dem muss ich das Kapitel verlesen!***" He called him an asshole and came to the school and reprimanded him for his actions. From that time on, Herr Schauer, obviously embarrassed by what had happened, gave me the best possible report card.

I was a dedicated student anyway, so I earned most of my good grades. However, I hated him from that time on. Ironically, he was my wife's favorite teacher and she was his star pupil. In the Fall of 2006 while visiting Echterdingen for the ***Krautfest*** (Sauerkraut Festival), Erné saw him walking in town. He was at least 90 years old then. When I saw him in return trips to Germany, I greeted him and shook his hand. I do not recall when it was that I forgave him.

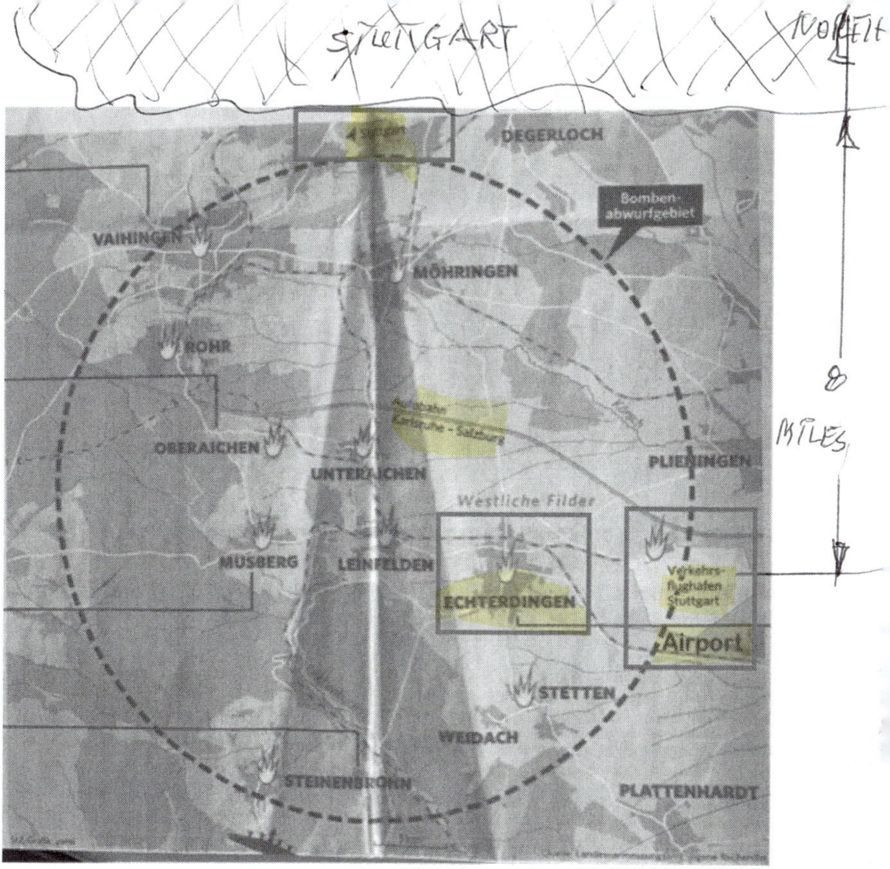

Destroyed towns and countryside in Stuttgart vicinity on March 14, 1944.[17]

CHAPTER 4

DREAMING OF AMERICA

***"Life is not a series of obstacles,
But, a journey full of exciting and limitless
possibilities!"*** ~ Eberhard Bulach

As a machine builder's apprentice, I worked 10-hour days from 7:00 a.m. to 5:30 p.m. with a 1⁄2 hour break for lunch. My weekly pay as an apprentice was DM 25.00 per 50-hour workweek (10 hours/day, 5 days/week). Many times we had to work overtime, up to 3 hours per day without additional compensation. My weekly paycheck barely covered streetcar fare for the week.

I woke up at 5:15 a.m. on workdays in order to eat a quick breakfast and leave at 5:40 a.m. to catch the 5:54 streetcar. It was a 1⁄2 mile sprint from my house, as I never walked. It got me to Ostheim by 6:50 and from there it was a 3-block walk to the factory. I was so happy to have a job that I was seldom late for work and never called in sick.

A buzzer sounded at 9:30 every morning and at 3:00 every afternoon for a 15-minute refreshment break for everyone. There were no drinking fountains, coffee or pop machines. But, there was a small canteen where beer, apple cider and pretzels could be purchased. My mother prepared sandwiches for my morning and lunch breaks. In the afternoon, I just drank mineral water. But, for the coffee and lunch breaks I drank a 1/3-liter of beer in a traditional flip-top bottle consumed at room temperature. Of course, I did not drink my entire bottle of beer during the breaks. I took periodic swallows to quench my thirst. One bottle would usually last from one break to the next.

The Keese Manufacturing Company had approximately 40 employees when I started working there. About 50% were veterans from the military who were employees of the company prior to their draft into the ***Wehrmacht*** (armed forces). Unskilled laborers were hired to cleanup the worksite and perform maintenance work. They replaced the employees who perished in the war. The company was allowed to employ 6 apprentices based on the percentage of employees. Since the horrible 5-year war cost the lives of almost half the skilled work force in Germany, the government subsidized the employment and education of apprentices in a 31⁄2-year program.

Manfred Schuster and I were the two first year apprentices hired by the Keese Mfg. Co. I soon found out that being a rookie apprentice was the worst job in the pecking order of an industrial plant like ours. Even the other 2nd and 3rd year apprentices picked on us and gave us some of their undesirable chores, among them: sweeping floors and cleaning bathrooms and shower stalls after working hours. Rarely was I ever home before 7:00

p.m. in the evening. This is what starting at the bottom is all about![18]

I didn't appreciate being harassed, but, thankfully, I kept my cool. This is mainly because I was so thankful to have this job; a job that would some day pay some of the top wages in the industry. It was a great learning experience. I continued to remind myself: Some day I will be some body and then I can dish it out and delegate as well. (If I so desired.) This was another period in my life when I "grew up quickly." Here I learned that patience is one of the greatest virtues a person can have.

The other five apprentices lived in Stuttgart, some even within walking distance of work. Since I commuted in from a farming community known for its rich soil for growing the famous ***Filderkraut*** (type of sauerkraut), my co-workers called me the "Filder farmer". I often became the convenient butt of their jokes.

As time progressed, I realized that because I was raised in a farm community I was accustomed to hard, hands-on work. I was not afraid to get my hands dirty. All of this gave me an advantage over the "city slicker" apprentices, who had to learn how to handle a hammer or shovel. Their hands became like raw meat when we had to stand by a workbench for one solid month using a file to make a perfect cube out of a hunk of steel. My hands were already calloused, therefore it did not take me long to finish my project. The apprentice coordinator noticed that I was not afraid to work hard or to use my God-given work ethic.

Workbench training was one of the most important facets of the apprenticeship program. The coordinator determined whether or not the first year apprentice had the necessary skill, patience and determination to become a top quality craftsman. About 25% of all new apprentices were eliminated during this process because of the lack of ***Fingerspitzengefühl***, natural ability combined with a healthy portion of patience and self-assurance, to do close tolerance work. In addition to instruction, we were responsible for taking apart, fixing and re-assembling tool machines that were damaged by the bombing raids. Even at that time, apprentices were the cheapest laborers in the work force because of their young age and assumed inexperience.

Erwin Bauer, a third year apprentice, and I were instructed to fix up a badly damaged "Hobel Machine" (shaper). He was the team leader. He constantly complained that as a third year apprentice he should not have to do this dirty and uninteresting work any longer. Before long our boss realized that there was a problem to correct. He made me team leader and assigned the other first year apprentice, Manfred Schuster, to me. Rolf, another apprentice, had to do our usual share of the cleaning because the boss could see that the new team was working well together, making great progress. In fact, we went on to re-work several other machines, which was not very clean work, but a terrific learning experience. It gave us the opportunity to custom make parts such as spindles or re-scrape the ways of the refurbished machines to put them back into production. Journeyman machinists normally completed this type of work.

This experience gave Manfred and me a leg up in the shop classes, which we attended twice each week at the

Jobst-Schule (vocational and technical school) in Stuttgart. Manfred and I were allowed to operate milling machines, lathes and grinders; machines assigned to the second and third year apprentices. We were envied by some of our other classmates, including some who worked at other companies such as Mercedes Benz in Untertürkheim.

A seed is planted! Uncle Gene and Aunt Florence Bulach visit Germany during Christmas 1947.

For several years during World War II, there was no contact between my parents and Uncle Gene. Mail traffic between the hostile countries was nearly impossible. Uncle Gene was worried about his siblings and other relatives. Since he was aware of the bombing and destruction of the German cities and transportation areas, he and Aunt Florence feared that their relatives may not have survived. His distress caused him many sleepless nights, terrible dreams and even nightmares. He was unaware that his brother had been captured by the Allies. After making mail contact with Uncle Gene in late 1945, we relayed the news that our house was totally destroyed and that father had returned home from the war physically and mentally spent.

As soon as American civilians were allowed to travel to Germany in the Fall of 1947, Uncle Gene, Aunt Florence, and cousin Ruth[19] (14 years old) came for a visit. They stayed for 5 weeks during the Christmas holidays. By that time, the German people had become accustomed to the presence of the American occupation forces. However, American tourists were still a sensation. The purchasing power of the U.S. dollar opened many doors and bought many scarce food items unavailable on the open market.

During their visit, we ate and drank like royalty and had many great parties. Uncle Gene was so happy that he found us all alive that he spared no expense to improve what seemed to be a very hopeless way of life. With the great devastation and piles of rubble dotting the German landscape around us, especially in the cities, he was amazed no one had been harmed physically.

At one of the dinners Uncle Gene sponsored in the Gasthaus Lamm, all the immediate relatives were treated to our very first sirloin steak accompanied by plenty of beer, wine, singing and ***Schaukeln*** (swaying). Father, who was still recovering from the starvation diet in Corsica, consumed far more alcohol than his system could endure and spent the next two days in bed penalized for his overindulgence.

During their visit, I had several discussions with Gene and Florence about the way of life in the United States compared to Germany. There was a mile wide gap in the standard of living between the two countries. I was fascinated with anything connected with the mighty USA, a country that seemed invincible; a country that, in my opinion, could do no wrong; a country that achieved the ultimate standard of living and freedom of choice for its citizens.

My hunger for information about the "strongest nation in the world" and "the world's liberator from destruction" grew daily. I visited the Stuttgart ***Amerika Haus*** founded by the U.S. military government. The America Houses in American occupation zones were centers where the German people could learn about American culture and politics, and engage in discussions to build a transatlantic relationship. Whenever I could scrape together enough money I bought a copy of the Saturday Evening Post. I bought it, not because I wished to read it cover-to-cover (I could not read English.), but because I was attracted to the cover illustrations by Norman Rockwell. Also, I liked the full-page colorful advertisements for the "Big Three" automakers.[20] I had visions of some day driving one of the pictured convertibles in the countryside depicted by Norman Rockwell.

As soon as Americans were allowed to mail packages to Germany, we received periodic "care packages" from the Bulachs and other distant relatives. I remember getting a pair of golf shoes because they were too small for my father. We thought the spikes were for walking on gravel pedestrian paths to control slipping. We had never heard of or even seen any golf played in our area. One of our relatives must have worked at Schmidt Brewing Co. because we received a long sleeved work style shirt with the Schmidt Brewing Co. logo on the back. I was proud to wear it because everyone commented on how different and very "American" the shirt was.

Before the Bulachs returned to the U.S., they promised to sponsor me to come to the United States. First, however, I needed to complete my apprenticeship as a machinist/tool & die maker. For a German citizen to emigrate to the U.S., they had to have a trade or profession in order to be employed. I was told at the

American Consulate that German craftsmen were in high demand in America's post-war industry. To satisfy my curiosity about my "promised land," I read every book or newspaper about the U.S. written in the German language. I prepared myself for the day I could set my foot on American soil with every ounce of my being.

I inquired about English classes at the Amerika Haus in Stuttgart. Beginning level English classes were offered only during the daytime working hours. So, the only exposure I had to the English language before coming to the U.S. was via an English-German dictionary, which I used to translate articles and advertising slogans in the Saturday Evening Post.

When a person wished to immigrate from a foreign country to the United States, a sponsor was required. This sponsor, often a relative, agreed to take on the legal obligation of financially supporting the applicant. My uncle, Eugene Bulach, came to the United States in 1924 under the sponsorship of his mother's brother, John Lorch. John and his brother, Georg, came from Hausen an der Lauchert in the Swabian alps region of Germany in the 1890s. They were both deceased by the time I arrived, but I did meet John's son, Ken Lorch. Ken had flown for the US military during WWII and shared personal stories with me.

Ken had bombed Northern Germany and had to abort his return and bail when his B-24 Liberator was shot down. He became a POW at a loosely guarded camp[21] in the Black Forest. He escaped to Switzerland and made it back to the United States. Ken retrained to fly the B-17s and flew back to England in order to fly more missions bombing Germany.

As Ken bombed the Mercedes and Bosch plants in Stuttgart, he was aware of the fact that he had relatives living in that area. It didn't seem to diminish his dedication to the military's mission that he had been assigned. Whenever I saw Ken after these stories, I always greeted him by saying, "Ken, I'm glad you missed me when you dropped your heavy loads, you son of a gun!" We shared war stories whenever we had the chance. He was also always amazed that the German intelligence continued to track him knowing his St. Paul address, the comings and goings of German visitors, and the immigration status of his entire family.

On September 29, 1951, the freighter "American Judge," a WWII Liberty ship owned by the United States Shipping Line, sailed from Rotterdam, Holland [the Netherlands] to its New York City, New York destination; a 7-day crossing of the Atlantic Ocean. This was my "voyage to the promised land."

My U.S. entry visa was valid for only 3 months and all spaces on the passenger liners were sold out. The only available tickets were on merchant ships, which were operated by the same shipping line as the passenger ships. Many of the merchant ships were equipped to handle up to 40 passengers.

Our Liberty ship could only accommodate 12 passengers, all male. The idea of making the Atlantic voyage on a freighter appealed to me, especially considering the $80 rebate from the normal passenger liner ticket. I knew that I would be reimbursing Uncle Gene for all of the pre-paid costs that I incurred ($2,000 sponsor bond and all travel costs), so this savings was beneficial.

The ship's accommodations were nothing fancy. We were housed in a 20'x20' single story box like structure. The area was designed to hold the ship's infirmary (located on the top of the aft deck), one shower stall, one urinal and one toilet bowl. We slept in double bunk beds pushed together against one side of a wall with a table and four chairs in one corner of the room. There were no shelves or lockers because these were temporary quarters. The room may have been a storage unit at one time or a place to quarantine an ill crew member. We just lived out of our suitcases, which we parked on top of our beds after they were made in the morning and stacked them in a corner at night before we went to bed. We took turns stacking the luggage, two people per day, because we had 12 different stacking techniques. Each person wanted his bag on top for easy access in an emergency

Communication was a challenge due to language. There were 4 Germans, 2 Americans, 2 Norwegians, 2 Belgians, 1 Frenchman and 1 Italian. It was decided that German would be the common language since one American, Richard Hess, could also speak fluent German. Our Norwegian and Belgian roommates didn't like that idea. They hated all Germans as a result of World War II and everything reminding them of Germany. (And who could blame them still only 6 years after the end of that awful war?)

Lester was the name of our African-American steward aka cabin boy assigned to keep our room clean, make the beds and assist us in any way possible. He even gave us a tour of the ship. Lester also showed us the crew's day room, which had a ping-pong table, two card tables, a small corner library with a sofa and two lounge chairs, and a record player with a cabinet full of American albums. We were allowed to use this room as long as members of the ship's crew were not using it.

The ship's captain invited us to join him for our 3 daily meals in the small dining room. Since he and his entire crew were American, our German language did not get us far. But, hand signs and body language were a good mode of communications when all else fails.

We departed Rotterdam during early nightfall on the 29th of September. The following morning, as the sun came up, we found ourselves in the British Channel heading west toward the Atlantic Ocean. Little did we know then that we would not see the sun for the rest of our voyage, which turned into a 10-day fiasco.

As the day progressed and we left the protection of the narrow channel, the winds picked up and the waves with huge white caps became more turbulent thereby rocking the ship in all directions. Some of our roommates were becoming seasick, occupying the bathroom or hugging tightly to a nearby wastebasket. Matters weren't helped any when Lester informed us that the Liberty ships had a structural design flaw. They had a history of breaking in half when fully loaded if waves exceeded 15 ft. And, we were fully loaded hauling chemical fertilizer to New York.

A huge storm was predicted over the North Atlantic Ocean. The captain explained to us at dinner that evening that we would be navigating around the storm so our travel time to our destination would be at least 2-3 days longer. Several from our room were already missing at the evening meal. As the seas became rougher during the night, only Richard Hess and I from the passenger hold were at breakfast the next morning. The ship's crew, minus Lester and the captain, seemed to be in full attendance.

Huge waves already washed over the deck. Richard and I timed the wave intervals in order to run the 40 ft. distance to the cabin while holding on to two ropes that had been strung from mid-ship to our cabin. When we arrived at our room, we found Lester cleaning up vomit from our violently ill cabin mates. The stench was horrendous. We opened the bulkhead doors for some fresh air, but that allowed water to come in, so we had to close them right away. Opening the four portholes on each side of the room didn't help either. Spray from the huge waves breaking against the ship blew in resulting in wet blankets on the bunk beds and drenched luggage in the corner of the room. Lester rolled his big dark eyes and, with sweat and tears rolling down his cheeks, predicted we would not reach New York if the storm grew any worse.

Lester left our room promising to bring wooden pallets on which to pile our luggage to keep them above the 3-4 inches of water sloshing across the floor. We actually never saw him again until we disembarked from the ship 10 days later. The ship's second officer let us know that Lester had become seasick and was confined to his cabin due to an emotional breakdown. He also informed us that we should not expect any service from any of his crew members. He had become shorthanded because 1/3 of his crew, including the captain, had become seasick.

Richard and I were given permission to care for our cabin mates and prepare toast in the kitchen. They must be forced to eat even if they throw up, he said. They also needed liquids so as not to become dehydrated. His last piece of advice was that we should tie ourselves to the ropes when we went to the midship and never go alone. If anyone got swept overboard, there would be no rescue possible. Our ship could not turn around against the huge waves. The ship needed to face the direction of the storm at all times.

Richard and I kept busy. We gathered pallets and rope to tie down our luggage. We also bailed water and fed our roommates toast or fruit or whatever they could keep down in their stomachs. We realized that we could not afford to get sick because if we did there would be no one to care for us. Each day there were fewer and fewer people in the mess hall at mealtimes. Richard and I took advantage of free run of the ship, the storeroom and the kitchen. We didn't live on toast. We ate Spam, bacon, eggs, pancakes and various canned fruits, and even ice cream. The liquor cabinet was under lock and key, however.

Everyone was hopeful that the storm would soon let up, calming the seas and allowing the sun to shine. One night on a kitchen run, Richard and I spotted the moon and a few stars poking through an unexpected break in the clouds. We brought back this report to our cabin and our roommates promptly jumped from their bunks to see this miracle themselves. We were all hopeful this was a sign of better weather ahead, but, alas, it was not to be. The weather did not improve until we reached the U.S. coastal waters along Long Island. During the final days of our voyage, two of our fellow passengers had to be tied to their bunks because they were so weak from a week of vomiting. They could not stand or eat without assistance. The ship's foghorn repeatedly blared an awful sound of foreboding. Even Richard and I were losing our youthful enthusiasm. The excitement of dealing with the unexpected and the adventure of being caught in a terrible storm on the high seas had lost its luster.

As we approached Long Island on the morning of October 10th, the sea seemed to recede slowly and the ship's constant motion calmed. At dusk, we could see the horizon for the first time and soon saw land. Words can hardly describe our exhilaration. Our patients began to perk up and began eating. They could again smile and joke, and the spark returned to their eyes. Though their pallor was still greyish-green, they could walk and care for themselves.

As we came closer to land, we could see the rotating beacon of a lighthouse. And, far off to the left there was a fixed light that became larger and brighter as we approached. It was Manhatten's brightly lit skyline framing the Statue of Liberty from behind. There she was, Lady Liberty with her right arm outstretched into the sky holding that beacon of light that signaled welcome to millions of immigrants as they arrived to their "promised land".

There were no dry eyes on board our ship. For a few moments, our Norwegian and Belgian travelers forgot political and ethnic barriers. We were brothers and members of a team who lived through 10 days of hell. We had arrived and we were alive! A tear still comes to my eye when I recall and savor the sweetness of that view and the relief of crossing the Atlantic alive.

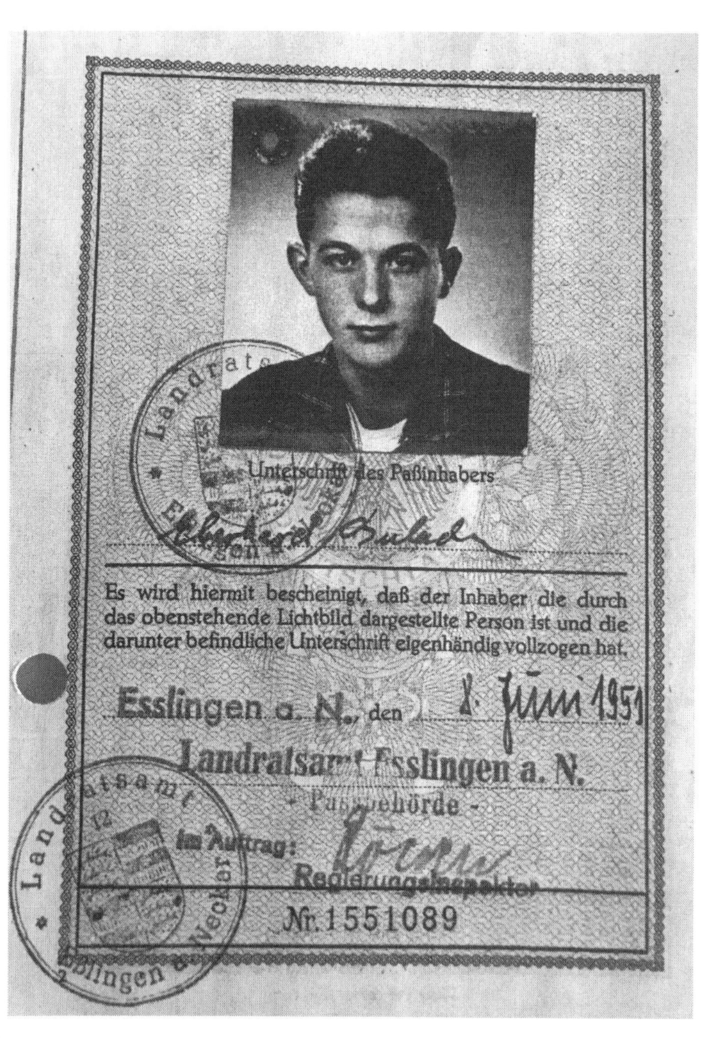

Unterschrift des Paßinhabers

Es wird hiermit bescheinigt, daß der Inhaber die durch das obenstehende Lichtbild dargestellte Person ist und die darunter befindliche Unterschrift eigenhändig vollzogen hat.

Esslingen a. N., den 8. Juni 1951

Landratsamt Esslingen a. N.

- Paßbehörde -

Im Auftrag:

Regierungsinspektor

Nr. 1551089

Eberhard's passport when leaving Germany.

CHAPTER 5

ARRIVAL IN THE UNITED STATES OF AMERICA

"Handwerk hat goldenen Boden."
~ Deutsche Weisheit

A trade in hand finds gold in every land.

Processing all immigrants to the United States at Ellis Island in the Upper New York Bay of the Hudson River was standard procedure in the years after WWII. However, since my ship came in 11:00 p.m. on October 11th and there was only a handful of people on the ship, we were allowed to proceed to the American Lines shipping dock along the East River in Manhattan. But, we were not allowed to leave the ship until properly screened by two immigration agents. That occurred around 1:00 a.m. on October 12th. Like Columbus many years earlier, I "discovered America" myself on that day.

We were required to pass a health physical plus accept and sign off on five major conditions:

1. You will assimilate to the American way of life.
2. You will make learning the English language a priority.
3. You will register for the draft.
4. You have proof of guaranteed employment upon arrival.
5. You have a guardian willing to provide a bond. (Due to my status as a minor.)

Once these questions were answered in the affirmative and proof of identity and employment were provided, we were permitted to take our "life changing steps" on to American soil.

All the other passengers had at least one person waiting for them at pickup. Richard Hess and I were the two exceptions. Richard was returning from a visit to his German grandparents. We made plans to take a train to Indianapolis the next day since there were no trains running during the Columbus Day holiday. The New York City subway trains were running, though. We sought out a hotel room for the night. The thought of sleeping in a clean, warm, cozy bed without the floor moving below us was quite appealing. Richard and I found rooms at the YMCA William Sloane House for 50¢ a night and it was located just a few blocks east of the Hudson River waterfront.

We were too excited to go to sleep. After we unpacked and cleaned up, we decided to have a meal in the cafeteria, which was open 24 hours. For 75¢ we could eat a hamburger and a hot fudge sundae. Outside the cafeteria, we spotted a shoeshine boy looking for work. At 3:00 a.m. we had our shoes shined for 10¢ each.

Richard and I decided then to walk the few blocks to Broadway. We were amazed at all the activity even at this time of night. And, oh, the people! We walked past a movie theater boasting a capacity of 2,000 people. This we had to see. So, we took in a movie at 4:00 in the morning. The movie title escapes me now, but I do recall we paid 15¢ for the movie and 10¢ for all the popcorn we could eat. (Popcorn was new to me and I have yet to acquire a taste for it.) More amazing than being in a huge movie theater early in the morning and eating popcorn was the fact that we were the only ones there besides a dozen or so stray cats. Apparently no one was concerned about wasting electricity or making money to pay for it.

We returned to the hotel and ate breakfast rather than going to bed. It was past 6:00 a.m. in Minnesota so Richard helped me make a collect call to Uncle Gene and Aunt Florence. I was concerned that they were wondering what happened to me since my scheduled arrival in St. Paul was for October 10.

I was correct, as the first thing out of Uncle Gene's mouth was, "Where have you been all this time?" Before I could respond, he chastised me for calling long distance, as it was so expensive. When I asked him how else I should have contacted him, he could only say that had I arrived on time, it would not have been a problem. As if to say that I could have prevented the delay.

Uncle Gene was not thrilled with my plan to go to the top of the Empire State Building while I was in New York City. I was told to get to St. Paul by Sunday night, October 14, because we had to go to work Monday morning. We agreed on the trains and arrival time in St. Paul. Nothing like putting a long hatpin into my euphoric bubble!

Richard and I parted company at Grand Central Station continuing our separate journeys west.

I reflect fondly on those incredible feelings of my first day in America. I was young and embarking on a new adventure, dazzled by the majesty and the glitter that was New York City. The experience was dramatic and life changing. I felt like I had been reborn into a new and better world. Germany was still recovering from its war torn status, so a life of nonchalant and easy excess in this new land was almost too much to absorb. It was overwhelming to think that the concept of "shortage" was nonexistent. Add to this the size and grandeur of the city. It was like starring in a Walt Disney movie.

I arrived in St. Paul, Minnesota at 10:00 p.m. Sunday, October 14th with 7 cents and a New York City subway token in my pocket. I was also thoroughly exhausted. The journey from Echterdingen, Germany to St. Paul, Minnesota, United States had taken 14 days.

Uncle Gene and Aunt Florence were at the train depot waiting for me. I don't remember if handshakes, hugs or pleasantries were exchanged. I do remember that the entire way home I received lectures from both sides regarding their inconvenience for going to the train station consecutively for six nights to find that their nephew was a "no show". I didn't realize at the time that they were actually relieved and glad that I had finally arrived safely. In their own way they were happy that I was there.

I was glad to arrive, finally, at the Bulach home and was ready to sleep. I was overwhelmed by the great comforts provided for me. I had my own bedroom with a walk-in closet, central heat and an attached bathroom with a shower. The room was in the basement with walls of knotty pine paneling and a great deal of privacy. For the first time in my life, I slept in a heated bedroom and had the luxury of warm water from the sink faucet for washing up and brushing my teeth. I felt like royalty or at least like a VIP. Did I really deserve all of this comfort?

My contemplative musings and carefree sleep didn't last long. At 6:00 a.m. Monday morning Aunt Florence's piercing voice came down to my basement bedroom with, "Sleepy head get up!" This jolted me out of bed and sent me upstairs for breakfast. Uncle Gene greeted me with, "We go to work in the morning at 7:00." I told them that I didn't have any work clothes with me. He told me that was not a problem because I could wear some of his clothes until we went shopping for some of my own, using my first paycheck, of course. This would be interesting since Uncle Gene was approximately 6 feet tall and weighed 220 lbs. I was about 5'8" and barely tipped the scale at 150 lbs. I could fit my entire body into one of his pant legs. His belt wrapped around my waist twice and his boots were four sizes too big. But, off I went to work with Uncle Gene.

Uncle Gene owned and operated a small construction company with three employees: Gilbert Motz, Lambert Motz, Don White. Their primary work was in residential concrete and an extra pair of hands was definitely needed to complete the scheduled work before the December freeze.

As the rookie and the youngest in the group in addition to not speaking English, I was designated the dirtiest and most unappealing jobs. My appearance probably didn't gain me any respect either. I felt like a bum in Uncle Gene's clothing and I knew that the children walking by on their way to and from school made fun of me. Finally, on Saturday, Uncle Gene took me shopping for work and dress clothes as well as shoes and work boots. We bought what he wanted, not what I liked. At least everything was new and fit better.

My starting wage was $1.00 per hour. However, I never saw the money. Aunt Florence charged me $25 per week for my room and board. The rest of the money she put into a savings account for me. I had to beg and plead for spending money. All my letters to Germany were mailed by regular mail, which took 2-3 weeks, as airmail stamps were considered too expensive and extravagant.

My seventeen year old "know it all" ego learned quickly who was in charge and who gave the "marching orders" as long as I lived under the Bulach roof.

It was decided during my second week in the Bulach home that we would no longer communicate in German. This was done so that I could learn English more quickly. I also enrolled in night classes for learning English at the St. Paul International Institute two times per week. On Wednesday, October 17th, Aunt Florence said, "Eberhard,

I am going to church for choir practice and you are coming with me." I told Aunt Florence I couldn't go because I couldn't speak English. She responded, "That is exactly why you are going." I soon learned that nobody said "no" to Aunt Florence without suffering a consequence. It took me quite some time before I agreed with her reasoning. In retrospect, I can see that my English did improve by leaps and bounds and my diction became clearer.

During the war and even after the war, it was difficult to be from Germany or speak the German language. Anything relating to Germany was ***streng verboten*** (strictly forbidden). I was afraid to open my mouth and speak to a stranger for fear of being called 'a Nazi'. It was different at St. Paul's Church.

As the first German immigrant following WWII to attend St. Paul's Evangelical and Reformed Church, I had celebrity status. I appreciated it very much, although it made me uncomfortable at times. I was amazed how quickly I was welcomed and accepted into our church family. Everyone, especially individuals of my age group, made it a mission to "Americanize" me as quickly as possible. It was this group that nicknamed me "Ebbie". To them, Eberhard was too difficult to say and sounded too much like a last name. Ebbie was more American.

Cousin Ruth assisted significantly in my cultural assimilation. As a junior at South St. Paul High School, she invited me to various school celebrations and dances. Ruth was also an active member of the church youth group and we often went to the fun activities together. Ruth was an expert typist and found a job with the State

Farm Insurance Company in St. Paul straight after high school graduation. She enjoyed dancing and wanted me to learn how to dance as well by fixing me up with some of her co-workers when they attended old time music dances at the Amerika Haus, Schlief's Little City or the Prom Ballroom. I arranged my own dates after her work transfer to Philadelphia.

In Germany, church activities at that time were reserved for Sundays only. I was surprised by the variety of groups and committees that met throughout the week to discuss church or social issues. One of the groups was the College and Career Club. It met regularly for lectures as well as social and sporting events. It included movie nights, scavenger hunts, canoe trips, swimming parties, overnights at the YMCA Camp St. Croix, paper drives, Palm Sunday worship attendance at Central Presbyterian Church on 10th St. and Cedar St. in St. Paul, house parties and many other events.

Dating among members of our age group was also acceptable practice I soon found out. I was encouraged to go on a "blind date" sometime. I was not very eager to pursue that idea, since I had concerns regarding entertaining an unsighted person. I could not take her to a movie for instance. What would I do with her seeing eye dog?

Going to my first outdoor movie was also an eye opening experience. Six of us in Carl's big 4-door Buick were counting our money for admission to the Roseville outdoor theater. We discovered that we had enough money for admission, but had no extra for popcorn and soft drinks. To solve this problem, two of us had to disappear into the car-trunk until we passed through the admission gate.

The lights of the car were turned off at dusk before the start of the feature. As the newcomer and one of the skinniest, I was volunteered for the trunk. I didn't expect to be imprisoned for almost 2 hours in that dark and very uncomfortable dungeon. Confined to these tight quarters with a kid with bad breath added to the punishment. We couldn't get out until our driver found a parking spot in the back row of the theater grounds. I caught on to their game and the next time we went to the drive-in, I brought enough cash to pay my admission and the driver's. Paying for the driver guaranteed me a legitimate back seat.

Going to strange houses and places, looking through stuffy and hot attics, smelly basements, chicken-coops, barns and vegetable gardens in search of items on a scavenger hunt list was also a new experience for me. Again, I was "the greenhorn" often not knowing what we were looking for. I found it nerve wracking and stupid. By the time I figured out what the game was all about, our group stopped doing this type of entertainment. Would I ever figure out this American culture?

Now, after 60 years of church and choir membership, I have only pleasant and positive memories of my membership at SPUCC. This membership experience shared with my spouse Erné over the last 50+ years molded me into the person I am today. I learned that it is more pleasant to give than to receive. Believing in God, our Christian faith and Christian values combined with a belief in my abilities, too, have been my trusted companions on my life's exciting journey thus far. Without the spiritual and moral support of my church family during the happy times and the difficult times along the way, I would not have been successful in reaching the goal I set for myself over 60 years ago: Fulfillment of the American dream! And for this, I am eternally grateful.

Soon after I arrived in St. Paul, Uncle Gene and Aunt Florence, my cousin Ruth and I visited Fred and Martha Remmele for supper. The Remmeles' daughters, Martha and Mary, were also there. They were younger than me by 1 and 2 years respectively. Fred and Uncle Gene met at the International Institute where they both took English classes. Both men came to St. Paul in 1924. Fred Remmele, founder and owner of Remmele Engineering, Inc., had agreed to give me a job when Uncle Gene decided to sponsor my immigration to the United States.

After the New Year in 1952, I began working at Remmele Engineering. Remmele Engineering was located at University Ave. and McKubin St. in St. Paul. I was fortunate that the machine shop was located on the University Avenue streetcar line that connected with the Annapolis streetcar line only a 1 mile walk (jog!) from Uncle Gene's house. I worked at Remmele Engineering in the wintertime as a machinist making parts for printing machinery and for Uncle Gene in the summertime doing construction work.

My punch card was number 11. I had the distinction of being the first in a long line of German immigrants hired by Remmele Engineering after WWII. The first immigrant hired after WWII was Hen-Rebane from Estonia. Fred Remmele hired only German immigrants who were journeymen machine builders and tool and die makers because of the expertise they brought to his machine shop and special machine divisions. He knew how well we learned the basics of quality workmanship. He had served as an apprentice as a tool and die maker in Germany after WWI before he emigrated to the U.S. in the mid-1920s.

The work was very interesting. In addition to learning English, I had to learn the English measuring system since I was accustomed to the metric system. The blueprints and machine calibrations were now in terms of inches instead of centimeters. As the youngest employee at Remmele Engineering, I did not do much machining at first. But, I soon realized how thorough and valuable my 31⁄2-year apprenticeship served me as a foundation for my future.

Remmele had a project where moving parts for particular machinery had to be scraped or filed to size by hand. This was a specialty process I had learned during my German apprenticeship. It was also something I enjoyed doing and the expertise came in very handy at Remmele because none of the other workers there had much experience in this area. This was a great boost for my self-confidence and good for my ego.

Most human beings can't recall taking their very first steps in their life when they were around one year old. I certainly can't. But I will never forget putting in my very first concrete steps in 1954 as a 20-year-old cement mason apprentice.

I was in my final year of a 3-year apprenticeship program working for my Uncle Gene. Uncle Gene and I decided that I should install a new 3-riser front entrance step on a new house for his friend on Butler Ave. in West St. Paul. This would be my uncle's version of a journeyman's exam to test my skills. The job included doing my own pick and shovel excavation for footings, setting up the proper forms, ordering, pouring and finishing the concrete. I would do this without his supervision and help. I would place the necessary 2 yards of ready-mix, finish the concrete and clean up the site.

The homeowner, Mr. Johnson, was a 3M retiree who watched my every move. He asked questions about my work, too. His constant questions brought an additional challenge as I was concentrating hard on each step of the process so I would not "screw up."

The ready mix truck came at the requested time. I took the time to double check the proper dimensions and the necessary procedures to secure and stabilize the concrete forms. Everything seemed to go according to plan. My "shadow" was encouraging me all the way and commenting how impressed he was of the fine job I was doing, considering that it was my very first solo job.

As I was finishing the sides of the 3-riser step, Uncle Gene drove up to check on my progress. As he walked up to the project, he pulled me aside and said, "Eberhard, your step looks very nice. But, you have to take it out because the bottoms of the side forms got pushed out due to too much pressure of the liquid mass of concrete against the sides of the forms. The sides of the steps are not perpendicular to the doorframe of the house. This happened because the forms did not have adequate bracing."

I stepped back about thirty feet from the steps and saw the obvious flaw. Standing in front of the work, I did not notice the problem. Uncle Gene gave me a choice: I could remove the fresh concrete with a pick today as it had not yet set up or I could wait until tomorrow and remove the concrete with a jackhammer. The jackhammer method would be much more time consuming. Furthermore, he continued, I would have to do the work on my own time and pay for the materials.

I almost cried and so did Mr. Johnson. As I walked to the truck to get a pick and a sledgehammer to start the demolition process, Mr. Johnson pleaded with Uncle Gene by telling him that he would plant some bushes alongside the new step anyway and no one would see the problem. He would also pay for the job right away. Uncle Gene would not agree. His response was this: "Eberhard has to learn to do the job right the first time!"

The following day I repeated the same process of the previous day. Re-using the same forms saved some precious time. Of course, I made doubly sure that the bracing of the forms was more than adequate this time. Thankfully, my second attempt passed Uncle Gene's inspection. Feeling sorry for my second attempt, Mr. Johnson slipped me a $20 bill with the promise not to tell Uncle Gene.

This very costly and humiliating experience taught me a lifelong lesson that served me well for many years.

Whenever I, or one of my employees, felt that the forms built were sufficiently secured, I advised them to add additional bracing to make sure that there would not be a costly failure. It's safe to say that it never has happened to me again. This costly lesson, no doubt, saved me many wasted hours of time and material costs on projects during my working life. The idea of paying for your mistakes to learn a life-enduring lesson is, sadly, not acceptable in todays' working environment!

In 1954 my cousin, Eugene Haegele, son of my father's sister, Rösle, asked Uncle Gene to sponsor him to come to St. Paul. He was 21 years old and did not need a guardian like I did. This made immigration issues less problematic for Uncle Gene and Aunt Florence. They considered this request seriously and thought that Eugene would be a good companion for me since he was only 13 months younger in age. Like me, when I arrived in St. Paul, Eugene did not know any English. The plan was that he, too, would work with us as a construction laborer until he learned English. After that he could work in his trade as an electrician.

Eugene was raised on a farm in Hausen an der Lauchert, a farming community 60 miles south of Stuttgart. Because of this experience, he disliked hard, physical work; thus the reason for taking on an electrician's apprenticeship in the city of Reutlingen. It turned out that working for Uncle Gene was not his cup of tea either. Adjusting to Aunt Florence's rigid house rules and discipline was a struggle for him as well. He was always the last one at breakfast in the morning and his bed was never made to Aunt Florence's standards. Breakfast in the Bulach household was served promptly at 6:00 a.m. daily, even on Sundays and holidays.

Eugene could not understand how I so willingly abided by the strict rules without protest. He told me once: "***Ich bin doch kein Sklave.***" (I am not a slave.) He was in constant agony while living under those conditions.

These circumstances hastened his decision to move to Chicago, about a year and a half later, where he enrolled in the DeVrey Institute to study electronics. While there, he drove a taxicab after school and on weekends to support himself. It was quite a gutsy undertaking as he knew no one in Chicago and he was still struggling with English.

He made it work and graduated from the Institute with a degree in electronics. Along the way, he became enamored with the real estate business. His goal was to go to work in a suit and tie and be in control of his own hours. He never wanted to work for a boss or get up early in the morning. Flexibility and independence is what he wanted. Eugene became quite successful in business and was well known in the restaurants and bars of the Lincolnwood area of Chicago.

Eugene reached retirement age on March 14, 1998. He lived life in the fast lane, just as he liked it. Sadly, his irregular work hours, chain smoking and alcohol consumption took its toll. Though successful in business, he was not quite as lucky with female companionship. Wife number five, Ophelia, became a widow with his untimely death on April 12, 1998. He had one daughter, Andrea, from Ingrid (wife #2).

CHAPTER 6

SOCIAL LIFE

"Wo man singt, da lass dich ruhig nieder, böse Menschen haben keine Lieder."
~ Johann Gottfried Seume

Where there is song, you may gather without worry, because wicked people have no songs.

My social life from 1951 to 1960 revolved around church functions and activities of the St. Paul Soccer Club. I joined the College and Career Club at church to get acquainted with more people my own age. The members of the College and Career Club met on Saturday or Sunday evenings as potluck events at the church or in homes with speakers and discussions of current events and religious topics. We had outings related to the seasons as well. They included one-day canoe trips on the St. Croix River from Taylors Falls to Stillwater, weekend camping trips to the YMCA Camp St. Croix, baseball games by the St. Paul Saints at Lexington Park, hockey games by the "Saints" (same name as the baseball team) at the St. Paul Auditorium and movies at a local cinema.

I dated young ladies who belonged to St. Paul's United Church of Christ. Some of them sang with me in the church choir. Other young ladies were from my English classes at the International Institute, where I met many young immigrants from Germany, Austria and other European countries.

I became a charter member of the St. Paul Soccer Club in 1952 under the sponsorship of local jeweler, Karl Zeglin. The soccer club held its initial meetings at the America House (called the German Haus prior to WWII) located on Rise and Aurora Streets. It was torn down in the mid-1950s to make room for the new State Highway Office Building as part of the capitol approach re-development.

We were all young and unattached immigrants eager to establish contact and find a common bond. Together, we enjoyed social gatherings while adjusting to the American way of life. Each weekend there were dances at the Prom Center, Stahl House and the America House. Young immigrants met and danced to familiar waltz, polka and schottische tunes played by Whoopee John, The Six Fat Dutchman and Frankie Yankovic. There were always plenty of cute young ladies of different nationalities eager to dance. Even in those days, many of the young men could not or chose not to dance. They were just "lookers."

One beautiful, balmy, starlit night after the band stopped playing, my friends (Karl, Steve, Margaret, Wanda and Sophie) and I decided to get some fresh air and walk home. We went first to Sophie's house on George St. near the Robert St. viaduct. Steve and I realized as we continued our walk toward South St. Paul along Concord St. to the homes of Karl, Margaret and Wanda, that every step in their direction meant we would have to double back to get ourselves home. It was suddenly not such a smart idea, but we had agreed to the plan and walked them home near downtown South St. Paul.

Steve and I then turned back reaching my house at 1251 MacArthur St., West St. Paul at 3:30 am. By that time we had covered 12 miles. Steve still had another 4 mile walk home to St. Clair Ave. near the foot of the Smith Ave. High Bridge. He arrived home by daybreak at 4:45 a.m. with blisters on his feet. Steve complained long after that night about our foolhardy long walk so late at night. I was more amused at his frustration the more he complained.

Steve and I had another similar escapade connected to dancing. Whenever we were too broke or too cheap to take young ladies dancing, we went to the Prom Ballroom for Thursday Singles Night. Even at that time, there were always more women than men at the dances. There were two large oval shaped couches at the edge of the dance floor. There was an unwritten rule that if you danced with the same girl more than two times or if you danced with her all evening long, you were obligated to escort her home after the last dance.

The young lady I danced with one evening was good looking, had a great personality and was a terrific dancer. She came to the dance with her brother. Before I offered to take her home, I had to check with Steve to be sure that he had a ride home. Steve, the handsome, fun loving, smooth- talking "salesman" talked his dance partner into driving him home. With Steve taken care of, I could ask Cynthia if she would like me to drive her home. She said "yes," but warned me that she lived in Hamel, a town "just north and west of Minneapolis." Again, this was a trip longer than I anticipated. I drove many miles west that night on University Ave. from St. Paul through Minneapolis to Golden Valley and on highway 55 through Plymouth soon passing cornfields, pastures and streets I had never seen or heard of before. I realized that I fell for another trap. But, at least I didn't have to walk!

At that time there were no freeways connecting the towns. Traffic lights and stop signs slowed driving every 6-8 blocks on city streets. Finally arriving in Hamel, I asked Cynthia if she could make me a cup of coffee or at least give me a cold drink of water before I turned around and headed home. She replied, "No, I'm sorry, but I don't want to wake my parents and little brother. Thanks for bringing me home. Good night, Ebbie." About two weeks later, I saw Cynthia at the Prom Ballroom, but avoided her. I learned my lesson about her.

There are certainly many places in the world that boast excellent hunting, fishing, camping and outdoor activities. I have found Minnesota is also a great place for these pastimes. Hunting, like so many other activities in American culture, was a brand new experience for me. I enjoyed this pastime very much and was eager to do more of it and learn all I could about it.

The construction season ended early in 1951 due to an early winter. That winter became one the snowiest winters in Minnesota history. Uncle Gene took me deer hunting in Holyoke, Minnesota. We hunted with his cousin Hermann Mader. Hermann was a second cousin to my father and Uncle Gene. He came to the U.S. in 1924. He and his wife, Harriet, owned a farm and considerable woodlands outside of Holyoke. Hermann worked at a foundry in Duluth full-time and farmed part-time. During that hunting season, he took a week off from work to hunt and to act as our unofficial guide. We paid room and board to stay at his house for the 8 days of the hunting season. Harriet was an excellent cook and she made sure we all felt at home and were well fed before and after our hunts.

Lambert and Gilbert Motz, employees of Uncle Gene, George and Adam "Butch" Zocher, neighbors employed by Uncle Gene during their college summer breaks, and William Schlozer, a family friend and fellow church member, were included in our hunting party.

Hermann lacked the patience to sit in a deer stand and wait for a deer to walk into view. He could be heard moving about in the forest underbrush and stepping on dry branches. He also cursed loudly when he fell over a hidden stump or tripped on a tree root. I don't recall if Hermann ever shot a deer, but he probably chased deer to other hunters in the wood.

As his houseguests, we humored his authority regarding deer hunting in his area. However, we city slickers came to know his area quite well over the years with the aid of aerial maps and compasses. Hermann never carried a compass and bellowed that he knew his own woods and farmland like the back of his hand.

Late one afternoon, Butch and I returned from one of our hunts stopping occasionally to listen to the noises of the forest. We suddenly heard huffing and puffing coming toward us. It was Hermann. In his accented English, he yelled to us asking us where we were going. We should be getting back to the farm and we were definitely walking in the wrong direction, so we had best follow him home.

Butch and I challenged Hermann, whoever returned home last would owe the others a drink. We proceeded on our course and Hermann took off in his selected direction. Butch and I walked approximately 50 yards when we heard Hermann shout in his thundering voice, "Dammit. Wait a minute. You whipper snappers are right!" He underscored his embarrassment with several sentences of cursing. I laughed and told him that if he didn't curse, he couldn't speak English.

Instead of being insulted, Hermann found my comment quite funny and he fell to the ground laughing as loud as he could, holding his considerable beer belly and rolling around. I guess he considered my statement a compliment because he could not wait to get home and tell his wife what had transpired. "Imagine, Harriet," he bellowed, "these greenhorns told me, on my land, that I was going the wrong way and that I couldn't speak English unless I cursed!" Each year that we returned to Holyoke, he reminded us of that day and broke out in laughter until his eyes teared up.

❖

Our annual deer hunting party changed significantly in 1957. The summer and fall had been unusually hot and dry and there was a state of high fire alert. We were at the Maders' just finishing one of Harriet's delicious and plentiful meals, sitting around the dining room table playing cards, watching TV and consuming Hermann's bountiful beer and liquor. We were aware of the extreme fire danger in the area and heard rumors of game wardens commandeering able bodied men to fight the forest fires. We were laughing and enjoying ourselves when Hermann noticed car headlights coming up the long driveway.

Hermann thought was a neighbor, but noticed the state license plate and state seal on the care door. The forest ranger or game warden was looking for hunters to help fight the fires. Hermann excitedly waved us all into hiding in the basement. He opened the door to a forest ranger requesting "all hands on deck" for patrolling a fire containment line being bulldozed as he was speaking. The ranger was checking in with all the farmers in the area to get assistance. Between the extra cars in the yard and the extra dishes and glassware on the table, there was no denying the fact that people were hiding in the basement. We were required to start within 2 hours of the ranger's visit.

We had to show our driver's licenses for identification. The forest ranger then took our hunting licenses. He informed us that we were now working for the State of Minnesota for the duration of our hunting trip. We would be paid 65 cents/hour. There were no pardonable excuses. If we could hunt, we could handle a pickax or a shovel.

We were handed our credentials and a temporary identification card with our social security number on it. The ranger would return soon with tools and instructions and a ride to the fire line. We were to dress warmly for the night and bring flashlights, but no rifles or guns.

The entire 8 days of this hunting trip was spent fighting fires in 8-10 hours shifts, alternating days and nights. We slept at the farmhouse after our shifts, but the DNR (Department of Natural Resources) provided us with food and beverage (no alcohol) while we were on the fire line. They had a mobile kitchen. We managed to keep the fires from jumping and expanding across our designated area of the fire line. The forest ranger reminded us that if the fire got out of control, it would consume us. That was incentive for us to keep working.

Although the daytime and nighttime temperatures hovered above freezing, we were never cold due to the physical activity. At times the wind drove sparks into the area we were patrolling and we had to work like crazy to stay in control of our assigned area. Once the wind died down at night, we could relax a bit, but still remaining alert while walking the line. We were all exhausted by the end of the week and glad to be going home. The fire danger didn't end until it finally snowed the following weekend. The hunting season was over!

We each applied for a refund of our unused $5.00 hunting license, but did not receive it. To make matters worse, I had purchased a brand new red wool hunting suit to last me for at least 10 seasons. I bought it at the Kennedy Sporting Goods store in downtown St. Paul for what was "big bucks" at that time. (Uncle Gene and Aunt

Florence thought I was being extravagant.) After fighting fires, my brand new suit looked as if it had been through combat, as it had large holes burned on both legs and arms. The remaining fabric took on a charcoal color instead of red. A check for $450 arrived in the mail. Payment for my time. It covered my $75 room and board at Maders, but did not cover the cost of my clothes.

This was another unforgettable life experience I am glad to have, but do not wish to repeat.

Hunting trips that took place after this saw much colder temperatures and often snow for tracking. Colder, snowier weather made it easier to get a deer. Sadly, Bill Schlozer died of a heart attack during our 1958 season as he was dragging his deer to the car. But, he died with a smile on his face. I was doing my 2-year military service at the time.

CHAPTER 7

RETURN TO GERMANY

"Sorge nicht um das was kommen wird, weine nicht um das was vergeht. Aber sorge dich nicht selbst zu verlieren, und weine, wenn du dahintreibst im Strome der Zeit, ohne den Himmel in dir zu tragen." ~ Friedrich Schleiermacher

Do not fret about what is to come or cry about what is lost. But, be concerned that you don't lose yourself and cry if you drift away in the current of time without heaven to support you from within.

Perhaps it was "puppy love" or "first love" that Else Walker and I shared after we graduated from grade school and started our respective apprenticeships at age 14. Else and I were not only playmates ever since childhood, we were constant companions on our walks to and from kindergarten and all 8 years of ***Volksschule***. I lived at Uhlandstrasse 13 and she lived across the street at No. 12. Else was the second of 5 children, as I was the second of 4 children.

Our generation of youth, who grew up during the pre-war and wartime years, assumed a variety of responsibilities with the expectation of working within the family structure of the time. As we grew older and matured into our teen-age years, we found less time and opportunity to play with the younger neighborhood children because we had chores and shopping to do so that the ***Hausfrauen*** (housewives) were free to perform the work typically done by the men in the family. During harvest time, especially, all hands, willing and unwilling, of every age were needed to keep people fed and homes in order. This was necessary due to the shortage of manpower with the military draft of all able-bodied men (cannon fodder!) as the war progressed. Else's father, Fritz Walker operated one of three nurseries in Echterdingen.

Whenever I was done with my chores around our house and garden, Ernst, Else's older brother, would spot me and recruit me for help at his house with his family. Somehow there was always a job waiting for me. At times, I resented not having any time for myself or for playing ball with other playmates. However, the reward of fruit and vegetables for my effort made it less painful. My mother also appreciated my help in providing food for the family.

Else started her 3 1⁄2-year florist apprenticeship at about the same time I began my tool & die making apprenticeship. Else worked about 2 blocks from the city hall at Eberhardstrasse 18 in downtown Stuttgart. My place of work was about 6 miles southeast from there. We were often on the same streetcar coming home from work in the evenings. I began work at 7:00 a.m. and she began at 8:00 a.m. so we never rode together in the morning. Over time, our relationship matured with our age.

My mother supported my interest in Else wholeheartedly. As far as she was concerned, Else was a saint. As the oldest girl in the family, she had to help raise her younger siblings, Hilde, Martha and Otto, while her mother was working behind the florist counter serving customers at their store. With her responsibilities, she was mature well beyond her young age. She was very conscientious, kind and helpful, yet a bit too serious for my liking. Her parents did not support her interest in me. However, they tolerated me because I was Ernst's close friend and "gopher." They preferred that Else find a young man interested in horticulture, who could marry into the family business.

On the Saturday prior to my trip to the U.S., my classmates (about 55 of them) arranged a going away dinner party at the local Waldhorn Hotel. Certain foods were still rationed at that time with some specialties only available on the black market. Every attendee paid for his/her own food and drinks. As guest of honor, I didn't have to pay a thing. We were 17 years old and of legal drinking age for alcoholic beverages. The lack of new currency kept us from over indulging in too much beer or wine. None of us had cars so reckless driving was not a concern. We celebrated until 4:00 a.m. As I remember, I told my classmates in my farewell speech that I might never see them again. If and when I did return to Echterdingen, I would throw a party for them at my expense.

Historically, the majority of our townsfolk who immigrated to the United States prior to WWII never returned home. This may have been due to lack of funds or the 6-year interruption by the war. An anti-German sentiment in the U.S. during the war years caused difficult social pressures on immigrants as well.

Uncle Gene and Aunt Florence decided to travel to Germany for Christmas in 1953 as Uncle Gene had not seen his mother since their first trip after the war in 1948 and his mother's health was failing. He also had three living sisters and two older brothers, including my father, to visit. They also wished to meet Else.

Uncle Gene and Aunt Florence were concerned that I was forgetting Else. They were convinced that she was waiting for me back in Germany and that I should bring her back to America after she became 21 years old. After meeting her on several occasions at the flower shop or socially at my parents' or her parents' homes, they were convinced that she was the perfect match for me.

Else turned 21 on October 10, 1954 so I decided to settle the issue and travel to Germany to spend Christmas and New Years 1955/56 with my parents, siblings, relatives and Else. After 3 years and 2 months in the U.S., I cashed in all my savings (around $1,500) and booked a round trip ticket via ocean liner back to Germany to visit my family for 3-months.

Uncle Gene and Aunt Florence were not pleased that I would be gone for a total of 4 months. It was a significant period of time and required using up all of my savings. Aunt Florence, in particular, suffered the most due to her frugal nature. It was because of her adept management of my earnings that I had saved so much money. Nevertheless, they understood that I had to close the book on my relationship with Else.

I traveled two days by Greyhound bus from St. Paul to New York City ($50 round trip). Then there was a 7-day sea voyage to Bremerhaven ending with a one-day train ride from Bremerhaven to Stuttgart. From New York City to Bremerhaven I traveled on the MS Gripsholm. Three months later on my return, the same ship was renamed the MS Berlin.[22] I wasn't thrilled about a long, tedious voyage and traveling with 500 "older" people in the tourist section. I resigned myself to sleeping and reading the entire trip.

I was assigned to a table with three older couples in their 50s and another younger man, Werner, who was about my age, also returning home for the first time after emigrating to the U.S. Next to our table was another table with seven young ladies traveling to Germany to meet their husbands or boyfriends who were stationed with the U.S. Army in the American Occupation Zone. These young women were in a celebratory mood.

Every evening after dinner, these young women met at the piano bar for the inexpensive drinks available after our ship reached the high seas. Some of the ladies were now able to consume alcohol and the strong German beer, as there was no age limit on alcohol consumption on German ships at that time. Werner and I had our hands full, celebrating, talking and dancing into the wee hours of the morning. As long as there were customers, there was no closing time at the bar. One night we celebrated until 5:00 a.m. Returning to our cabins, we stopped at the ship's bakery to eat freshly baked hard and sweet rolls for breakfast before turning in and sleeping until lunchtime. What I feared to be a boring voyage became a festive week of celebration.

Upon arrival in Bremerhaven, I became the unofficial tour guide and assistant for four of the ladies whose husband or boyfriend had been unable to meet them at the dock. I got them something to eat, got them oriented in their new surroundings and got them boarded on their connecting trains. Providing this aid caused me to miss the first two trains to Stuttgart. One woman remained as my travel companion since her final destination was Patch Barracks outside of Stuttgart.

We watched a lot of German scenery out our train window during the 10-hour ride south and I explained about the houses, tile roofs, fences and other note-worthy cultural trivia. The red roof tile came from the clay of southern Germany. The fences and neatly trimmed hedges denoted property lines. Very few farmhouses were in the countryside like in the U.S. Her observations reminded me of my first days in the U.S.

Else was the only one in Echterdingen who knew the specific date of my arrival, but not the exact train. She waited patiently at each train from Frankfurt until I arrived. I was not expecting her, but was elated to see her.

We loaded my luggage in her brother's pickup and drove the 20-minute ride home.

I unloaded my bags inside my parents' front gate while she parked her brother's truck and then we went for a walk around the moonlit neighborhood. We had so much to discuss and catch up on. It had been such a long wait and here we were together again, finally. The clouds that had settled over our long distance romance disappeared into memory. I was glad I made the trip home.

Unbeknownst to me, my father had the late night streetcar shift the night I arrived home. While I was on my walk with Else, he noticed the suitcases in the front yard, read the luggage tags and realized that I had arrived. When I returned home, father was waiting for me in the kitchen reading a book. He did not want to wait until morning to surprise my mother, Gisela or Fritzle so we jolted them out of bed. Mother was speechless and could only cry. Gisela and Fritzle were upset that they had been woken up.

Since I was staying with my parents, I tried to be as helpful as possible by doing chores around the house and in the big yard when I wasn't visiting friends and family. The time in Germany was beneficial and educational on many levels. By the end of the three months I was ready to return to Minnesota. I knew where I belonged and where I would build my future.

During the 3-months that I was in Echterdingen, I saw Else only once or twice each week because of her long work hours during the holiday season making flower arrangements, Christmas decorations and gravesite wreaths at her family store. We were forced to meet secretly on many occasions because her father and brothers did not grant her time off to meet with me. I did not like sneaking around as we were doing so I went to her father one day to let him know of our plans to have Else come with me to America to see if she would like to live there and marry me.

Herr Walker was quite annoyed and accused me of "having the guts to come from America to kidnap his daughter knowing full well Else was a vital part of the family's business operation." He did propose that he would allow us to marry provided I learn the flower business and allow him to build us a flower shop by the cemetery. Ernst also opposed to our marriage in America because he would lose all the work that Else did for him and his dominance over her. My answer to Herr Walker in front of Else was that I would return to the U.S. with or without Else. It was her choice. By that time I was convinced that she was married to her family and their business and not in love with me.

Her reward for family loyalty was being overworked, underpaid, unappreciated and leading a solitary life. For the $1,500.00 it cost me to find out where I fit into Else's life I could have bought a brand new car in 1955. In retrospect, it was money well spent for the lesson I learned.

During a trip back to Echterdingen in the early 1970s, Herr Walker approached me admitting that he should not have stood in his daughter's way to choose a different life. His selfishness had created a life of unhappiness for her. My sister, Gisela, worked for her in the flower shop and learned that Else regretted her decision to stay behind. Else died December 13, 2013.

To this day, I am married to the true love of my life and ***Schatz***, Erné, for more than 60 years now! How interesting it is the way our paths go in life.

It didn't take long for me to realize that the U.S. and St. Paul, MN was my new home. I had a humble beginning in the job world, but I could tell that I could have a great future if I applied myself. Opportunities were everywhere. All I had to do was "roll up my sleeves and get to work."

I knew that my mother would be heartbroken to learn that I would stay in the U.S. She was sure that homesickness would eventually cause me to return to Germany. I realize now that it was wishful thinking on her part because she missed me. My mother's influence during the war years cemented a bond that could not be broken. She helped me become strong and tenacious and also taught me to be considerate and caring. How my thoughts, words and deeds affected my fellow human beings was, and still is, important. I cherished my mother always for these traits.

The war had instilled a spirit of independence in me. However, when I first broached my father with the subject of emigration to the United States, he was not in favor of my decision. He said, "No son of mine is going to become a gangster or a capitalist, if I can help it." In 1951 he didn't believe that I had the courage or stamina to carve out a new life for myself somewhere other than Germany. It was his attitude that subconsciously made me even more determined to succeed. My father and I did not have a close relationship and I rebelled against his authoritarian manner, the intimidation and the control that he had over the family.

I try not to be critical of my father since I don't know the type of childhood he had. I never knew my grandfathers. My paternal grandfather died in 1932, two years before I was born. My maternal grandfather died in the killing fields of Flanders, France in 1918 just before the end of WWI.

I do know that my father was hired out at the age of 14 to haul logs and merchandise with a team of horses for a cartage company. He also worked at the famous Lichtenstein castle as a ***Fuhrmann*** (wagoner). Since he came from a poor farming family, money was very tight. His parents could not afford to send him to school or to learn a trade. He had to earn money and turn his paycheck over to his father. I have been told that he was a very good student in grade school and that the principal wanted him to become a teacher. However, the family could not afford tuition and they needed his paycheck.

Father was always bitter that he never had the chance for an education. As an adult, he was well read and informed. He loved to read and to travel. Thankfully, in his retirement, he could afford to travel to satisfy his inquisitive mind to some degree. He did come to the U.S. twice, no longer objecting to his son's emigration.

CHAPTER 8

MILITARY LIFE

"Ask not what your country can do for you. Ask what you can do for your country."
~ President John F. Kennedy

Prior to Christmas 1956, I received notice from "Uncle Sam" that I had been selected to serve in the United States army for a "2 year vacation all expenses paid." I became U.S. Government property serial number US55568616. I could have asked for a deferment since my citizenship application was still in process. However, I was proud to be asked to serve my new adopted country and I decided to go sooner rather than later. So, I reported to the historic Dakota County courthouse in Hastings, MN for a physical and pre-induction meeting. Several years later, President John F Kennedy articulated how I felt at this time in my life.

I have heard it said that serving in the U.S. armed forces "is a great experience for a young person" or "will either make or break a young person." Both statements are true. Fortunately, the majority of young recruits made it a positive character building experience. But, I did see some of my fellow recruits completely self-destruct. For many it was the first time away from home and therefore an overwhelming and dramatic event. In the military, we lost our human identity and were reminded constantly that we were government property identifiable by our serial number, not our name.

On December 17, 1956, I boarded a train with 30 other men from the Minneapolis draft board headed to Camp Chaffee, Arkansas. We all speculated on the surprises we would find upon our arrival there. We found the rumors that Camp Chaffee was a cold mud hole to be true. Temperatures hovered barely above freezing, which caused much misery.

Another physical inspection awaited us here; the infamous ‘short arm’ per army slang. We recruits were instructed to line up in single file, turn 180°, drop our drawers, bend over, and spread our cheeks; an unsettling request to most for the lack of privacy and modesty.

Barely recovering from that ordeal, we then walked the gauntlet where nurses, both male and female, poked us with two huge needles in each arm. I don’t recall the type of vaccinations we received. From there we were marched in formation to the barbershop to receive a 2-minute white wall haircut, assembly style. Hippie style long hair on men was just becoming popular, so there was a lot of hair that fell to the ground and long faces over the loss on their heads. Now, we all looked like the ugly, unsmiling faces of a police lineup posted on the post office bulletin board.

Several days later we were marched to the quartermaster barracks during a heavy downpour to receive our army issue duffle bag of uniforms, underwear, socks and boots. The supply room sergeant behind the counter sized us up and handed us our package. There was a tailor shop at the Post for alterations that could be done at our own expense, of course.

We were fed three square meals each day in a large mess hall capable of serving 3,000 soldiers at one time. While going through the chow line wasn't going to get us mom's home cooking, the food was edible. Meals were consumed in 15 minutes, too, because another soldier was standing behind you to take your seat. It was interesting for me see a correlation between team players and system fighters by how much food was left on a persons tray. Training sessions and other disciplined activities also differentiated the soldier's personality.

Our newly formed company of 200 men was flown to Fort Ord, California to make room for more recruits coming in to Camp Chaffee. Fort Ord already had a nicer ring to its name and we knew for sure that the climate in California would be decidedly better, even during the rainy season. The sunshine after the rain always gave a more positive light to our situation. Located along the coast of the Pacific Ocean just north of the Monterey Peninsula, the soil around Fort Ord was sandy rather than the sticky, heavy loam of Arkansas.

Fort Ord distinguished itself further in marching style. We no longer had conventional walking or marching outside of our barracks. Every move was marked in double time to improve endurance and physical agility. Basic training consisted of close order marching drills, learning different commands and formations (while wearing full field gear with steel helmets and carrying our designated weapons). Classroom sessions taught warfare, military tactics, 'Army Code of Conduct', memorization and aptitude tests. Field stripping and reassembling M-1 rifles was also taught. This skill goal was a time of 45 seconds, eventually done while blindfolded.

Soldiers unable to perform the required drills had to practice their skills and timing after supper when the rest were off-duty. They had to repeat the full drills until they passed the test. These were marked men. When the drill sergeant needed a scapegoat or volunteers for KP or latrine duty, these men were called upon first. Basic training in the U.S. army was a picnic for me compared to the discipline of the Hitler Jungvolk. I was then thankful for some benefit of my past experience.

I completed my first 12 weeks of Basic Training at Fort Ord as a rifleman on a sniper squad. I always tried to be a good soldier, follow orders and not fight the military system. It was easy to see that the boys who fought the system had trouble and pulled extra guard or KP duties. I did have my own trouble the second day at Fort Ord.

I was one of 15 men from my unit assigned to KP duty. I was scrubbing pots and pans with 3 other men from a different unit. As we were talking and joking around, one guy, noticing my accent, asked where I was from. I told him I was from Germany and right away he said, "You must have been a Nazi." As diplomatically as possible, I said that I was only 11 years old when WWII ended and that I, too, was a war victim. Our house had been bombed and we all practically starved to death. I was now wearing the uniform of the United States of America and had nothing to do with Hitler. And, I resented being called a Nazi.

Just to test me, the guy called me a Nazi again just a few minutes later. I got angry, lost my cool and punched him in the nose. He fell backwards into a sink. He wanted to fight back, but two other guys restrained him and called the mess sergeant who gave us a lecture and sent the other guy to the infirmary to look after his bleeding nose. The next day I was ordered to see the company commander.

Captain Johnson read me the riot act and told me he could punish me for assault under Article 15 of the Army Code of Conduct. The other man, Milton Cohen, of Jewish descent from Brooklyn, had filed a complaint. After hearing my side of the story, he summoned Milton to his office. He sat us down to analyze the incident being careful not to take sides. He understood that I had suffered under Hitler and his regime just as the Jewish people had suffered. He understood that I also wore the U.S. uniform to counteract some of this past history. I should not have thrown the punch and Milton should not have called me a Nazi. We were to promise that this would not happen again. We shook hands and called the case closed. Since Milton belonged to a different unit, I didn't see him often after that episode. However, we did wave to one another if we did see each other on the grounds.

We had several company formations everyday. The first one was at 5:30 a.m., the second one was after breakfast, the third one was after lunch and the fourth one was at 5:00 p.m. when taps was played. Our first sergeant made it a game to make as many of the 250 men do 10, 20, 30 or more pushups in front of the company as punishment for infractions such as: uniform not completely buttoned, dirty boots, last man in formation, incomplete shave or smiling in the ranks. We were supposed to be "mean fighting men."

Smiling was not allowed. One of his favorite expressions was: "Wipe that smile off your face!" If he needed someone to pick on he would ask, "Is there anyone here who likes the army?" If someone raised his hand, that person would have to do 20 pushups. "You're supposed to hate the army!" He often looked straight at me and asked, "Bulach, do you like the army?" He knew I would say yes. "Good. Give me 10 (or 20) pushups." The sergeant would stand and count them off. After I returned to the ranks, he would ask me again, "Bulach, do you still like the army?" If I said yes, which I usually did, I had to do 20 more pushups.

In those days, I was in good physical shape. I know I could have done 100 pushups easily. One time I counted off in German and the entire company laughed out loud. That cost me another 20 pushups. After formation dismissal, he called me over and ordered me never to count off in German again.

Jim Cosgrove from South St. Paul was a recruit with me. He was always in trouble. He hated to get up in the morning and he cared little for punctuality or a neat appearance. We shared a double bunk. I slept on the upper bunk. It was my job to pull him out of bed after I returned from my early morning shower and shave. I was always the first one out of bed because I didn't want to wait in line for a washbasin and mirror, nor did I want to clean the sink before I used it. Not everyone was conscientious about cleaning up their mess. Jim called me "Tiger" because of my "gung ho" attitude. The name stuck with me during the first period of Basic Training.

After Basic Training, the entire company received a 2-week furlough. I flew back to St. Paul out of San Francisco on a Northwest Orient Airlines DC-7 4-engine prop plane. I sat between a young mother and her 4-month-old baby and an older, well-dressed gentleman. I wore my army dress uniform.

We experienced turbulence as we flew over the Rocky Mountains. The lady at the window seat felt nauseous and asked me to hold her baby. She began to throw up. The gentleman to my right reached for a bag soon after that. To my left and to my right they continued to vomit. I could only pray that I wouldn't get sick myself. The stewardess came with additional bags and removed the used ones. She was surprised that I remained strong between them. Meanwhile, the baby slept through it all and I prayed that I wouldn't throw up on the baby or my dress uniform. After landing, I carried the baby to the baggage claim while the mother carried her other carry on luggage and diaper bag. Thank goodness the young woman's husband was waiting for his family.

I returned to Ford Ord in early April for Advanced Training. At this time each recruit received his MOS

(Military Occupation Serial Number) or specialty classification. Mine was Chaplain's Assistant, MOS No. 718-10. I recognized only a few faces from the first 12 weeks of Basic Training at the first formation of Phase II. Our original group had been divided and sent to different forts for further training: Fort Sill, Oklahoma for artillery, Fort Carson, Colorado and Fort Riley, Kansas for tank and motor pool training.

Master Sergeant Soldato asked for volunteers for certain jobs or details at the first company formation. He needed a guidon bearer.[23] No experience was necessary. However, the person had to know how to march and keep cadence. I raised my hand because no other hands were raised. The soldier to my right kicked me with his left foot while whispering under his breath, "You dummy, nobody volunteers in this army?" It was too late.[24]

Sergeant Soldato acknowledged my hand and asked me, "What makes you think you know how to march?" My instant response without thinking was, "Hitler taught me!" There was snickering in the ranks as the sergeant stared at me as though he didn't hear correctly. He asked again, "Who taught you?" This time I responded by saying that I had learned in the Jungvolk. "O.K. smart ass," he shouted. "Front and center of the whole formation and show me what you can do. And, this better be good."

He handed me the company guidon and gave me a few quick instructions. I had to respond to his commands by raising and lowering the flag and turning left or right or forward and reverse as he counted out the cadence and commands in his booming voice. The rest of the company watched and listened at "parade rest."

Slowly I began to realize that I had made a mistake by opening my big mouth. I set myself up to be embarrassed in front of about 200 soldiers. Sweat ran down my face and neck as I concentrated and synchronized his commands with my steps and flag movements. Finally, after 5 minutes, which seemed like hours, he told me I could have the job; unless someone else in the ranks thought they could do it better. There were no other volunteers.

I became the guidon bearer for the next 12-week period. I met criticism and was called a "brown nose" by my fellow recruits, especially when they learned that I was now exempt from latrine, KP and guard duties because I had to take care of the company flag and polish the brass pole daily while also practicing commands with the officers of our company. Because I was expected to be the first one on the parade grounds for every formation (assembly), I was allowed to be among the first in the chow line right after the non-commissioned officers. The officers ate separately.

Although I was expected to have a clean and pressed uniform with polished brass buttons and spit shined boots, the flag job was a "gravy job." As long as I was in this army for 2 years, I challenged myself to be the best damn soldier I could be and get the most out of the experience. My objective was to know how to take care of myself and not to be a burden to the soldier next to me in the fox hole should we find ourselves in combat. This attitude helped me time and time again during my military experience.

As a sniper, I had to attend every target practice for each company of the regiment to ensure that my shooting eye and trigger finger were in good form. Several days after the marching event, I had some additional good fortune on the rifle range while our marksmanship was tested with the firing of the standard issue M-1 rifle.[25]

We practiced zeroing in on our assigned weapon from 100, 200 and 300 yards distance while in prone, sitting, kneeling and standing positions. Our weapons, we were told, were our best friends. They were to be pampered and cleaned every day, just like we take care of our bodies. As an infantry rifle man, it was of utmost importance to learn the proper breathing technique and squeezing of the trigger. The goal was to hit our target with the first round of ammunition because a second shot was never guaranteed. The practice with air rifles and .22 rifles during the Jungvolk years was my advantage. Gun handling, safety, breathing technique and shooting came second nature to me.

As the day progressed, I had the sense that I was doing well. I was working for the Expert Rifle badge by hauling down a series of bull's eyes. I noticed that my platoon leader Lt. Harper paid special attention to my score as he was walking back and forth on the firing line with 40 positions. Our company commander Capt. Johnson also made the rounds and stopped to confer with Lt. Harper. Not too far downwind from them I could hear Lt. Harper comment about the ex-Hitler youth shooting the bull's eyes out of his target. At the end of the day, I was informed that I had attained the highest overall score for the entire company. The full impact of the day's events didn't sink in until I was in bed that night. The actual scores were not posted until the next day.

My chest swelled with pride when the announcement came at reveille formation that Pvt. Bulach had earned a 3-day pass for attaining the highest target shooting score, 223 out of a possible 250 points. I reported to Capt. Johnson's office for the pass, two weekend nights reserved at the magnificent Mark Hopkins Hotel in San Francisco. Capt. Johnson was interested in knowing what it was that made ex-Hitler youth such good soldiers. There were two other German immigrants my age in different companies of our regiment who also performed well. I thanked him for the compliment, but told him that I did not want to be characterized as an "ex-Hitler youth." I was wearing the U.S. Army uniform as a matter of choice since I was not yet a U.S. citizen. He apologized and promised the name would not come up again.

During my three days of relaxation, I enjoyed my first prime rib steak at the famous 'Top of the Mark' restaurant, visited Golden Gate Park, walked across the Golden Gate Bridge and rode the cable car from Market St. to Fisherman's Wharf. At that time, riders helped the trolley operator push the turntable for the return trip. Since I was in uniform, the ride was free.

Another memorable experience occurred when we were marching to the Fort Ord rifle range. The rifle range was approximately 3 miles from our barracks. All units generally marched to and from practice. We marched at the regular marching tempo for one mile, double timed the second mile and returned to the regular marching tempo for the third mile. We did this while wearing a steel helmet, a canteen, an ammunition belt and an M-1 rifle all together totaling +20 pounds. When marching regular time, the M-1 was slung over the shoulder. When marching double time, the M-1 was carried at port arms.

We were returning from practice on a cold and rainy day jogging double time all the way back to the barracks. I carried the guidon at port arms and kept my M-1 slung over my shoulder. The straps were too loose causing the trigger housing to crash into my back at each step. My clothes were soaked through from the rain and the continuous pounding of the trigger housing tore a hole through my clothes to the skin. I felt horrible pain, but couldn't stop to adjust the shoulder straps with the thundering pack of men behind me. Nearing the end of the march someone hollered behind me, "Bulach, you're bleeding!"

Back at the barracks I assessed the damage and found a 4-inch square area on my back bloody and shredded like hamburger meat. I went to the infirmary to get bandaged up. The wound healed in about a week, but my spinal column hurt for quite some time after that. Our first sergeant was very considerate and didn't make us double time until after the wound healed. He also allowed me to put 2 old socks over the trigger housing to soften the impact. This helped greatly.

I completed my advanced training at Fort Ord at the end of June 1958. At that time I received orders to report to the U.S. Army terminal in Oakland, California for transfer to Korea for 18- months of deployment.

During the late 1950s and early 1960s approximately 400,000 U.S. troops were stationed in Europe. The majority of troops were deployed to Germany. Because I was from Germany and still had family there, I was hoping to be stationed in Germany to be near them. I thought that my fluency in German would be advantageous. However, I was told that the troop quota going to Germany was full. The only way I could get there was to extend my tour of duty to 3 years. If I did that, they would send me to the army language school in Monterey, California for 6 months to learn a Slavic language. By that time I would have my U.S. citizenship. I could get the security clearance to become an interpreter at a military court in Germany. It sounded enticing, but since I had never been to Korea, I decided to let the chips fall where they may.

I boarded a troop transport with 2,000 other men at the Presidio in the San Francisco harbor. Our destination was Korea after a 24-day sea voyage. We passed under the imposing Golden Gate Bridge setting out into the Pacific Ocean. At suppertime on the second day of our voyage, the ship hit some rough waves and we were literally rocking back and forth. There was a sudden stampede of men running from the mess hall line toward the 55-gallon cans at the room's perimeter. Within minutes I was fifth in line instead of 300th with so many hugging the cans and vomiting. Unfortunately for those of us left standing, we had to clean up the hallways and bathrooms after our seasick comrades. We soon succumbed to the stench as well. We were stuck in our cramped quarters, 5-6 men on fold out bunks fastened against a wall with only 18 inches of vertical space between each bunk. We were unable to escape to go topside for fresh air. That was "off limits" for fear of men being swept overboard. I recall wondering if I could take another 22 days of this unpleasantness.

Mercifully, on the sixth day, we approached the Hawaiian Islands in calm waters. We were now allowed to go to the top deck in two-hour shifts. We were informed that the ship would stop in Pearl Harbor to take on fuel and provisions. All army personnel were allowed to go on land for 8 hours before continuing to the Far East. News also came that 130 men would be staying in Hawaii. I was one of these fortunate men.

It was almost embarrassing to disembark the troop transport knowing that the rest of the men had another 18 days of travel ahead of them to Korea. I could feel their envy. I was unaware at the time that this next 18 months would we one of the most challenging, yet happy, and character building periods of my life thus far. I never dreamed I would have the good fortune of spending this time in "paradise," the most popular vacation spot in the world at that time.

I was assigned to the 35th Infantry Battle Group (CACTI) of the 25th Infantry Division at Schofield Barracks. We lived in Quad A, a complex of 4, 3-story housing units. One company was composed of up to 250 men. A paved road ran in front of the barracks and a large grassy area was in the center used for formations. The area was off limits to foot traffic except for parades.[26]

We spent the initial weeks improving our marching and shooting skills as well as becoming acquainted with the men of our platoon and company. These men were our companions and the people on whom we would depend in time of war. I was assigned to the sniper squad of Company "C". This assignment required a great deal of target practice. I arrived too late for the guidon job so took my turn at KP and guard duties.

I attended the general protestant worship at the area "A" chapel conducted by Chaplain Harry A. Hataway on Sundays. Chaplain Hataway always had a smile on his face and kept his sermons short. He also interspersed real life experiences and humor in his message.

At one of his services, Chaplain Hataway announced that his chaplain assistant was rotating to the mainland and he was accepting applications from within the regiment for a replacement. Anyone with piano or organ and typewriter skills could apply. I thought that would be a fabulous job, but I didn't have the prerequisite skills. Nevertheless, I approached him with two other men after the service to express my interest in the position.

He asked my MOS since I didn't have the other skills. His face lit up when I told him I was a sniper. Chaplain Hataway told me that excellent marksmanship was also an important attribute that he had not mentioned. There were enough people in his congregation who could play piano or organ, and one could learn to type by attending night school on base. He requested my "bio" and I dropped it off quickly after our meeting.

I was summoned to Chaplain Hataway's office a few days later. There were five qualified applicants with musical skill and even seminary experience. However, I had the best marksmanship score and he liked the way I wore my uniform, always proper with shined brass and boots. He also liked my positive attitude. The job was mine if I wanted it. I accepted the job on the spot. We shook hands and he took care of my transfer to headquarters company. Since I now worked on Sundays, my day off was on Wednesdays. This was another lucky break because I took a chance and "stuck my neck out." I remember being told, "A turtle, when it moves forward, has to stick its neck out."

At headquarters company, I had to make two formations daily, reveille in the morning and taps at the end of the workday. Otherwise, there were no parades, no inspections, no KP and no guard duty! My peers accused me of riding a gravy train. Of course I had other duties and responsibilities, too.

My main responsibility was to be Captain Hataway's all around gopher and driver. I had to be available to drive the chaplain to the hospital for sick visits or take his wife shopping. At times on my day off, I was asked to babysit his children, Harry, Ray and Karen, or cut the grass at his officer quarters on base. Chaplain Hataway was not very handy and didn't like house or yard work. I also typed the Sunday bulletin, the monthly reports, kept the appointment calendar, and kept his jeep clean and serviced. I also was responsible for keeping the area "A" chapel and grounds tidy and clean. I shared these duties with the assistant to Catholic Monsignor Burns, Joe

Salerno. Joe and I decided to alternate these duties on a monthly basis.

Chaplain Hataway placed great value in my high marksmanship and that it was higher than Joe's. He deemed that his jeep was cleaner and shinier than that of Monsignor Burns and that the chapel and grounds were neater when it was my turn, too. I made sure that my uniform always looked sharp with my brass and boots brightly polished. As time went on, I became known for my dependability and Monsignor Burns even called upon me for some important appointments. I took my job seriously and wanted to be a credit to Chaplain Hataway. I was honored and indebted to him for choosing me as his assistant.

The 25th Infantry Division was training for tropical warfare at the time I was attached to them. Each battle group spent 2 weeks in the Kahuku Mountains Training Area for Jungle Training. It is a mountain range along the northeastern side of Oahu near what is the area of the present day (2014) Polynesian Culture Center. Kahuku had a tropical rain forest environment and temperature. The purpose of the training was to become acclimated to jungle conditions and live off the fruits and roots in the event we were cut off from supply lines. This was serious business as far as I was concerned. If ever I should be in that position, I wanted to be sure I was a survivor, just as I was during WWII. We didn't get any food for our exercise. We were given only toilet paper and water purification pills.

We lived off the wild fruits (banana, guava, mango, papaya) and the taro roots (the same root from which

Hawaiian poi is made). We all shed several pounds during those weeks. Some never finished the session. About one third of our group was transferred back to Schofield for medical or emotional reasons. It was certainly the trial that separated the men from the boys so to speak. Here was another instance where my past had prepared me well. I did not find this exercise to be of any hardship. In fact, I enjoyed the 2 weeks.

In addition to gathering our own food, we lived in 2 man pup tents. The two chaplains shared a large command tent where they also conducted services. One corner of the tent was partitioned off for the chaplains. Chaplain Hataway hated sleeping in tents (a reminder of his infantry days during the Korean Conflict) and found several excuses for not spending the night in Kahuku, thereby returning to his family at night. Monsignor Burns returned to Schofield every third night to say mass. He would return at 8:30 p.m. with a six-pack of beer. He and I would play chess. Joe sat in his tent because he didn't play chess.

While at Kahuku, we had a map reading course. We were split into 2-man teams. Starting from different positions, our goal was to assemble everyone at one end point. Captain Hataway and I were one team. Our experiences of hunting, army training and war combined got us to ground zero first. The Chaplain was so thrilled with our performance that he told everyone, including the company commander: "If we ever go into combat, my assistant and I will lead the charge!"

❖

Shortly after our Kahuku jungle training, Chaplain Hataway received orders to transfer to Fort Shafter, the U.S. Army Pacific Headquarters outside of Honolulu. Initially I was unable to transfer with him. However, "Chappy" Hataway was never one to take "no" for an answer. Colonel Henry, the division chaplain, owed him a favor so made the joint transfer happen. The battle group commander did not want to let me go for several reasons: 1. I had made Soldier of the Month for the entire CACTI Battle Group. 2. I wrote an essay, "My Job Protecting America's Freedom", and won an award from the Freedom Foundation of Valley Forge (a bronze plaque). Col. O'Malley told Chaplain Hataway that he didn't want to lose one of his best soldiers. This, at least, was the chaplain's story.

Duty at Fort Shafter (USAPAC Headquarters) was an entirely different experience compared to Schofield Barracks. It was relaxed and almost like a country club. Army officers with the rank of colonel to 3 star generals spent their final tour of duty here with a comfortable desk job before retirement. At Fort Shafter there were more officers than enlisted men. My right arm became sore from saluting all the officers above master sergeant as I walked around the post. Schofield was a training facility as well as the home base for the 25th Infantry Division, which from 1957 to 1959 was the only U.S. army division trained for tropical warfare outside of the marines.[27]

At Fort Shafter, because it was an administrative base only, we were allowed to wear the Bermuda uniform given to us upon arrival in Hawaii. The uniform consisted of above the knee Bermuda shorts, short sleeved shirt, knee high socks and army dress shoes (no boots). We were cautioned to use a lot of sunscreen lotion because as "property of Uncle Sam", we were not allowed to be sunburned. Sunburned appearance or a sunburn requiring treatment causing exemption of daily duties was an offense punishable by Article 15 of the Military Code of Justice. Duty at Fort Shafter felt like a normal 8 a.m. to 5 p.m. job in the civilian world. The Military Police (MP) performed guard duty and civilian employees performed KP duty. There were no inspections and no morning or evening formations. Also, there were no bed checks or morning head counts. Each person was responsible for timely completion of his own job assignments. This schedule allowed me to pursue my own interests and activities after 5:00 p.m. each day.

I didn't miss any chow time meals, though. With an army pay of $90 per month, I could not afford to eat out very often. The cost of living in Hawaii, even at that time, was very high. Chaplain Hataway frequently invited me to his home, a furnished bungalow on post, for supper and I always accepted gratefully. Mrs. Hataway was a good cook. After supper, I took their kids to a nearby playground to play before bedtime. While babysitting, I even had a lesson in diaper changing. It was not part of my MOS, but I was willing to learn and it was a small price to pay for the privileges I enjoyed as a chaplain assistant.

I was assigned to the post chapel with four other assistants. Lt. Col. Fred Jewell was the senior chaplain.

His assistant was career soldier, Nabuo Miamoto.[28] We maintained chapels and attended to Sunday worship services at Fort Shafter, Fort DeRussy (Waikiki Beach), Fort Kamehameha (Pearl Harbor), and Fort Ruger (Diamond Head). As the lowest ranking assistant, I got the jobs none of the others wanted.

I was in charge of maintaining the four staff cars and one jeep plus the four chapels. Once each week, I was given a 5-man detail to clean the chapels, cut the lawn, trim the shrubs and manage other associated tasks. Some of my paperwork was delegated to Margaret Melandish, a civilian employee performing secretarial duties for all of the chaplains.

My job on Sundays was to arrange the altar for Protestant worship services since the chapel alternated each hour between the Protestant, Catholic and Lutheran denominations. The chapel needed to be cleaned and the altar flowers needed to be fresh. As the assistant, I printed the order of worship on the bulletin available to the congregation as they entered. Once the service started, I closed the doors and positioned myself in the rear of the chapel to assist any latecomers.

Chaplain Hataway usually asked for my feedback regarding his selection of music in addition to the length and content of his sermon. As I grew to know him better, I became more comfortable telling him if he rambled. His plan was to speak 8-10 minutes. In the event that he couldn't reach a conclusion, I was to stand up in the last pew to indicate that his 10 minutes was up. Only once, when he was full of fire and brimstone, did he embarrass me by saying, "Ebbie, sit down. I barely scratched the surface of my comments."

During the summer vacation months, our chaplains, along with parent volunteers, conducted Vacation Bible School. The Vacation Bible Schools rotated among our four facilities with a two-week session each. During one of those sessions, I was driving back to the main chapel in Honolulu to pick up supplies and blacked out while driving our brand new 1957 Chevrolet staff car. When I awoke, I found myself in a patient room at Tripler Army Hospital, one of the largest in the world.[29]

I rammed head on into a telephone pole. Since this preceded the era of airbags, seatbelts and padded steering wheels, my face took quite a beating. I had a total of 27 stitches and was kept in the hospital for one week for tests and observation. The doctors never determined the cause of the blackout.

This incident has always remained a mystery to me, too. It never happened before and has never happened since. The chaplain and I were quite concerned that I would lose my army driver's license. However, since the tests came out inconclusive, I was allowed to drive again after two weeks. The telephone pole I hit snapped off on impact and cost Uncle Sam $700 to the City of Honolulu. All wooden poles on the island were imported from the mainland, so the cost was quite high.

When I made my daily rounds to check on the chapels and water the flowers and shrubs, I always allowed myself enough time to take a dip at the Fort DeRussy Beach. I often found myself with female company, especially on my Wednesday day off, because the other

G.I., sailor, marine and air force personnel were at their daytime duty post. There was an hourly bus service from Fort Shafter to Waikiki Beach. However, it was more convenient to use a staff car or a jeep from the motor pool as long as I wore my uniform on my off day. I kept "civvies" at the chapel's office as well as towels and swimming trunks. From the Fort DeRussy Chapel, it was a 2-minute walk to the beach. The staff car had to be returned to the base by 10 p.m. when the gates were closed. Although there was one gate staffed by an MP in the event of emergencies or other situations. License plates HQ 12, 13, 14 were assigned to the chaplain's office and were waved through by the guards. Since Fort Shafter was purely an administrative site, no combat troops were seen. Only military police manned the gates screening authorized vehicles entering this highly secure area.

There are individuals in our lives, including parents, teachers and siblings, who leave footprints on our hearts and influence our minds. They are people, who in some way helped us discover our potential by challenging us or broadening our horizons. Chaplain Harry R. Hataway is one of these people for me. He is one of the most unforgettable human beings I have ever met.

Chaplain Hataway was a man of small stature, barely 5 ft. 6 in. But, he had a large personality. He had a high-pitched tenor voice and a great laugh. Because of his small size, he took short, but quick steps to keep up with everyone else. He was always talking or whistling unless something went against his “graw” as he was known to say when he was in a bad mood. Chaplain Hataway had a loud voice, so we could always tell where he was. He was not an early riser, therefore was seldom in the office before 9:00 a.m.

Margaret Melandish and I found ourselves covering for him in the early hours. When the chaplain arrived, he came up the steps to the Fort Shafter Chapel humming a tune or whistling. He set his briefcase on his desk, fetched a Reader’s Digest magazine and disappeared in the rear of the chapel for a 1/2 hour of reflection or positive thinking in the restroom. When he reappeared singing loudly or whistling, “Onward Christian Soldiers” or “Happy Days are Here Again”, we knew all went well. When we heard “Rock of Ages” or “There is a Balm in Gilead”, the day would be long and tedious.

One day he stomped in from his back office grinning from ear to ear. He stopped me and said in a very serious tone, “You know Ebbie, the most overrated thing in the world is a piece of ass! And, the most underrated thing is a good, healthy sh—t!” I was stunned to hear such words coming out of the clergyman’s mouth and stood in disbelief. He had always conducted himself in perfect decorum, polite and proper. Only on a few occasions when we were in the field with the “boys” on maneuvers did he revert back to his infantry army days in Korea.

The wartime experience had prompted him to devote his future life to Christ. Once discharged, Chaplain Hataway entered college and then seminary. He was the troops because he could joke and relate to the days of a "dogface recruit". He could tell a story or BS as well as anyone and he earned the nickname "Chappy".

Chappy and I hit it off from the start. We were both dedicated to our jobs and position in the army, yet we always appreciated a good laugh and making military life as fun as possible. He had a profound influence on my military life and much of that influence I carried into civilian life. It was Chaplain Hataway who, along with Corporal Eldon Hartman, served as my character witness on April 10, 1958 when I appeared before Federal Judge Frank McLaughlin of the Hawaii Territory to be sworn in with 66 other applicants to become United States Citizens. I recall seeing a tear roll down his cheek as the entire group recited the Pledge of Allegiance. The Pledge was followed by the Star Spangled Banner.

Chaplain Hataway passed away February 3, 2003 in Many, Louisiana at the age of 79. He and his wife, Cleo, settled in Louisiana after retirement to be near their four children and several grandchildren. I stayed in touch with them over the years and visited them on two occasions when Erné and I attended conferences in New Orleans.

Berti Witt from Cleveland, OH was another German immigrant and soldier, like me, stationed at Fort Shafter. He was the General's driver. He invited me to join a folk dance group that met each Wednesday at a church in Waikiki. I wished for more contact with the civilian world so accepted his invitation. I liked the diverse group of people and joined. I became quite active in the club and became proficient in several of the folk dances.

My partner, Jeannie Anderson, and I were scheduled to perform an Austrian dance called the ***Zillertaler Ländler*** on Hawaiian television as a promotion for International Week at the International Market Place. I asked Aunt Florence to mail me my ***Lederhosen*** with ***Trachtenjanker*** and appropriate shoes, socks and ***Tiroler Hut*** for the occasion. Since Jeannie had a ***Dirndl***,[30] we became the designated ***Tanzpaar*** (dance couple). She was graceful and light on her feet.

Jeannie and I started spending more time together outside of the folk dance group by taking her children on picnics and camping on the beach. At Hanauma Bay, the swimming and snorkeling was especially good. It didn't bother me at first that she was 12 years my senior and a divorcee with two children until I noticed that the children were becoming attached to me. I started to back off on the friendship. Jeannie was bright and well educated and had many good qualities, but I was not interested in a long-term serious relationship. Conscription had interrupted my life once, as a duty to my adopted country. I had to stay focused on my life goals.

I am proud to be a third generation soldier fighting for my country. My father served dutifully during WWII in Hitler's army while suffering great hardship during battle and additionally while in captivity. But, fortunately, he did come home to his family. And, for that, we are thankful.

My maternal grandfather served in WWI in Kaiser Wilhem II's army and gave his life on the battlefields of Flanders Fields in southern Belgium only a few months before Armistice Day.[31] Grandfather, Wilhelm Hertfelder, knew that his return home was highly unlikely and felt compelled to write a letter to his children offering his advice for their lives without him. The original handwritten letter is among family documents in Germany, but a photocopy has been passed on to me. Its translation is presented here.

Echterdingen, 3 August 1918

To my dear children!

Since I must go to war, I feel responsible for giving you some advice for life's journey.
Remain honest, sincere, go to church faithfully and practice your Christian faith. Treat you mother with respect and kindness and don't give her any arguments. Support her with all her work and don't be lazy. Strive to achieve the qualities of your parents so that in your later years you will reach your goals.
In the event that I do not return, please live up to my advice. Be kind to your mother once you are married.
I wish you a good life. Auf Wiedersehen!

Your father, Wilhelm

Three generations of Bulach men in military uniform.
Top: Son, Eberhard, Middle: Father, Fritz Bulach,
Bottom: Grandfather, Wilhem Hertfelder

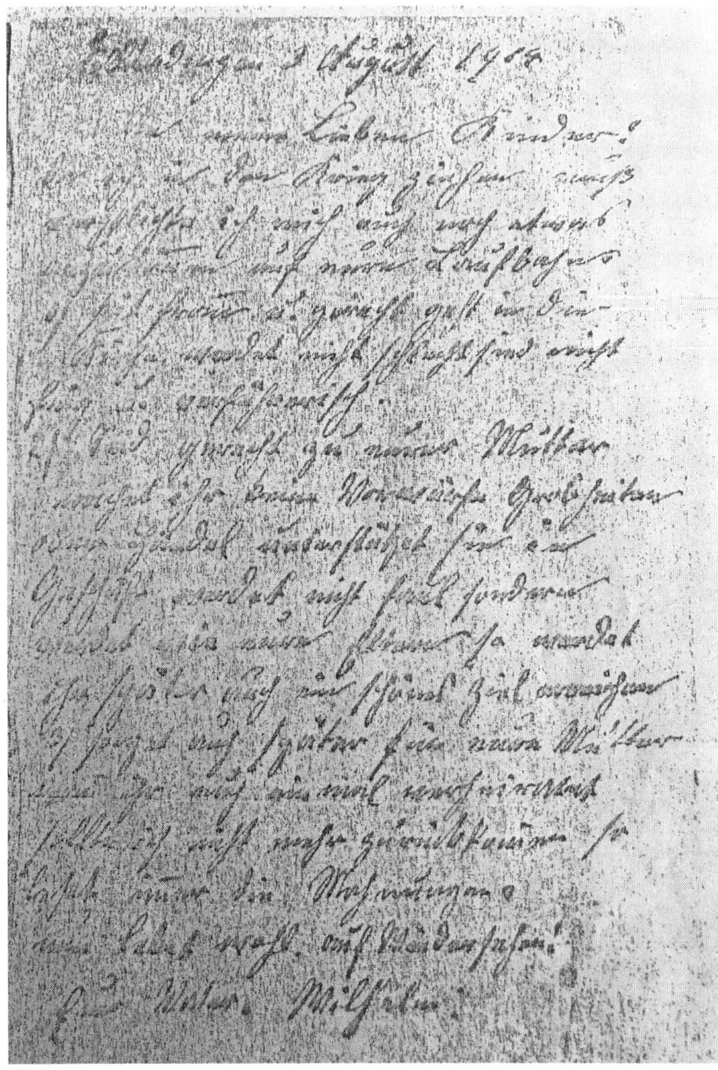

Photocopy of Wilhelm Hertfelder's letter to his children before going to war.

Guide-On Flag Bearer

Chaplains' office staff 1958: Eberhard, Monsignor Burns, Tom Moore, Margaret Melandish, Joe Salerno

Chaplain’s Assistant at Fort Shafter

Jungle training – Kahuku Mountains, Hawaii

CHAPTER 9

CIVILIAN LIFE

"Jeder ist seines Glückes Schmied!"
~ Appius Claudius Caecus

Every man is the architect of his own fortune.

My draft into the military was December 17, 1956, which meant that my 2-year obligation would end just before Christmas 1958. One option to return home was to take the troop ship back to the mainland for discharge. Chaplain Hataway was not eager to lose his assistant right before the Christmas holy days, one of his busiest church seasons. He did not want to train a new assistant and I, personally, did not like the idea of traveling on another ship. Ending earlier would have been good, but also would have meant spending Christmas on the ship somewhere at sea. As a second option, Chaplain Hataway offered to arrange for a MATS flight (Military Air Transport Service) to San Francisco after January 1, 1959.

Although it extended my discharge date by 3 weeks, I thought it was a good plan.

However, the New Year's flight from Hickam Air Force Base did not work out as planned. I was bumped off three flights due to military personnel of higher rank. Once I arrived at the Oakland Army Terminal, I had to wait an additional 10 days for my discharge papers to catch up to me since I was not discharged with my original group. [32]Had I taken the troop transport, I would have been discharged on December 28.

I finally made it back to St. Paul where the temperature was -20°F. I didn't mind, though, because I was glad to be back in what I considered "God's Country". I was also ready to implement my 5-year plan. There was plenty of time during my military term to reflect on and make new goals for the future. However, my grandiose self-absorbed work plans became rearranged when Erné Kehrer entered my life the very next day on January 19.

My sister Gisela had come to live with Uncle Gene and Aunt Florence in March 1957, three months after I left for the army. Since it took at least one year to acquire a resident alien visa to the United States, we didn't want to cancel or postpone her arrival. Gisela attended Henry Sibley High School to perfect her English language skills and to receive her high school diploma. She worked part-time at the First National Bank in downtown St. Paul in order to pay her room and board. Gisela's boyfriend, Helmut Schwarz, was also living in New Jersey at the time of her arrival in St. Paul.

Erné Kehrer was Gisela's close friend and classmate from Echterdingen. Erné came to the U.S. in July 1958 sponsored by her relatives, August and Anna Entgelmeier, in Lehigh, Iowa, a small farming community. While living with her relatives, Erné worked for her room and board by doing house chores and helping in the fields. Since the farm was situated 24 miles southeast of Fort Dodge, the nearest town, there was no opportunity for her to go to night school to learn English. Her only contact with the larger social community was going to church on Sundays or riding along on shopping trips. Her uncle kept a detailed list of expenditures such as stamps for letters to Germany, clothing and toiletries that were invoiced to Erné once she found a job.

Erné came for a weekend visit to St. Paul while her aunt and uncle visited their daughter in Menomonie, Wisconsin. While Erné and Gisela were discussing her aspirations regarding work and learning English, the Bulachs invited Erné to stay with them as a way to accomplish her goals more quickly while living in a more urban environment. Gisela and Erné were thrilled with the idea and pitched it to August and Anna upon their return from Wisconsin. August and Anna agreed that it was a good plan for Erné's future. Cousin Ruth had already moved to Philadelphia, so there was plenty of room in the house.

Gisela was working the day Erné came to St. Paul so Aunt Florence requested that I go along to the bus station to pick up Erné. In my mind I remembered the 11-year-old little girl who played with my sister, wore pigtails in her hair and had a cute mischievous smile. Of course that was 8 years earlier when I left Germany. I didn't expect the tall, vivacious, blue-eyed blonde lady to step off the bus. Erné captured my attention at this very moment. My, had she grown up! (***Erné, Mensch, bist du aber gewachsen!***) This day is forever imprinted in my memory.

Once Erné got settled, she began attending night school at the International Institute to learn English and she found a job as a seamstress doing embroidery at the Lohman Company in downtown St. Paul, which was famous for making altar coverings and vestments for catholic and protestant clergy. That job required only the ability to do delicate handiwork, which Erné, as a tailor's daughter, had learned well.

Re-adjusting to civilian life in the familiar surroundings of the Bulach household and the community was easier than I expected. The bigger adjustment was living in the same house with two beautiful young ladies, Erné and Gisela. They intruded into my basement domain when they needed to fetch something from the freezer in the fruit cellar for cooking or to do laundry. But, I got over it quickly since it was now their job to clean my bedroom and bathroom on weekends.

Between Aunt Florence, Gisela and me, there were plenty of willing tutors to assist Erné with her English homework. Aunt Florence also made each of us read out of the 'Upper Room' magazine every morning. She would interrupt us constantly to correct our pronunciation. This embarrassed us considerably, especially the girls, who were often close to tears. We soon realized that Aunt Florence meant well and we learned a lot by her method, if only she had been a little more tactful in her criticism. Even Uncle Gene, who arrived in the United States at the age of 20, did not escape an occasional critique. He responded by saying, “Okay, Ma.”

I often felt sorry for the girls when Aunt Florence ordered them around or scolded them for not completing a job to her satisfaction. Aunt Florence seldom gave them a compliment. As long as they lived under her roof, she expected them to live up to her stringent expectations. I was seldom picked on. Perhaps, I had developed a thick skin in the 5 years I had lived with the Bulachs prior to my stint in the Army. I could play her game even though I did not always agree with her methods or live up to her expectations.

There were strict rules on bathing in the Bulach household. The two girls had to bathe together with only about 8” of water in the tub in order to conserve water. They soaked their underwear at the same time. I was told not to take a shower longer than 2 minutes, which was adequate for me. To my knowledge I was never timed. While I was in the military, I grew accustomed to showers less than two minutes in length.

The Bulach home was far from the city sewer and water supply when they built it in 1948. They had a well and were always concerned about running out of well water. It never happened, but there was certainly a mindset of scarcity that came out of conditions in Germany after World War I and the Depression of the 1930s. Having come from conditions in Germany after World War II, Gisela and Erné found it to be an inconsequential request. A bathtub alone was a luxury.

I often spent evenings going out with friends from church. Kay Koch and I had become good friends before I went into the army. We corresponded back and forth during those two years and her mother mailed me mouthwatering fruitcakes wrapped in rum moistened cheesecloth for Christmas. As soon as I opened those tins, the smell in my locker gave away the scrumptious contents and I was asked to share that delicacy with my roommates (about 12 to 15 men in a squad room). That fruitcake never made it to Christmas. It barely lasted longer than one day.

During the summer, our household of five settled into a routine of work and play. Uncle Gene and Aunt Florence loved having young people around the house. It created a great deal of fun and excitement as long as it was in good taste and according to their rules. We were allowed to invite some friends over for parties on the lawn in good weather or in the basement when the weather was unfavorable. We enjoyed singing German folk songs. Even Aunt Florence, who was born of German parents on a farm near Hershey, Wisconsin, knew all of the songs and all of the verses. Aunt Florence cooked and baked. She could make a delicious, yet simple, meal in short order out of the vegetables she raised and the wild game and fish we hunted; cooking mostly on her combination wood cooking and heating stove.

Sunday had its own rhythm. We still had breakfast at 6:30 a.m. regardless of Saturday night's late activity, which had a 1:00 a.m. curfew. Even at 25 years old, I had to obey that rule. We all went to church. Uncle Gene and the girls sat in the balcony, while Aunt Florence and I sat behind the altar with the choir. Sunday afternoons we visited friends or friends of the Bulachs' extensive circle came by for a visit.

My job as a machinist at Remmele Engineering was waiting for me upon my return from the army. I was permitted, also, to work as many overtime hours as I wished. This really made my financial picture a lot brighter. Fred Remmele continued to encourage me to register for classes in the mechanical engineering department at the University of Minnesota. He also proposed to pay at least half of my tuition if I committed to full-time employment with him. I could work for him during the summer and winter breaks, and work weekends and the night shift to earn spending money. That was an appealing proposition, so I proceeded to register for fall classes at the university.

By early May 1959, Uncle Gene started cranking up his sidewalk, curb and gutter business. He expected me to grab my toolbox at Remmele and come work for him as a cement mason foreman in the summer as I had done prior to my military service. The wages in construction, especially with a union shop, were significantly high in those years. Also, Uncle Gene paid me a foreman's wage.

I still had many questions to address about my future. What path should I take for my career? Should I stay with Uncle Gene and take over his business when he retired in 4 years as he proposed? Should I take Mr. Remmele's offer of an education and a lifetime of work indoors? There was also the blue-eyed young lady living in our house. Did I want her to return to Germany when she earned enough money for a return flight, as she planned? Did I want to rethink my timeline for marriage? Time was a great healer. But, a decision was necessary by September and the fall school semester for both Mr. Remmele and Uncle Gene.

The lure of the warm spring weather and sunshine was too great a draw. In spite of Mr. Remmele's generous carrot, I laced up my size 9 Red Wing work boots and set to work shoveling dirt and concrete getting my body and biceps back in shape.

I could sense that Uncle Gene and Aunt Florence were eager that I pay attention to Erné. They suggested strongly that I take Erné to the annual Winter Carnival Parade in St. Paul on the last weekend in January 1959. It was a bitter cold day with a clear blue sky. Gisela had to work and Aunt Florence deemed the weather too cold for her to go out. Aunt Florence gave Erné her full-length fur coat to wear. This was our first official date. (I have a short Super 8 video of that day.) The weather was terribly cold as we stomped our feet to keep warm and I explained the meaning and activities of the floats and marching groups passing by on the street. Though Erné was freezing and miserable, she never complained and asked to be taken home because she knew that I wanted to see the entire parade. Her stamina and pride became evident.

Erné's 19th birthday was on March 1, 1959. We celebrated among the five of us at home with a good supper, homemade apple pie and a glass of "Virginia Dare", a sickly sweet wine that was a favorite of Uncle Gene and Aunt Florence. Gisela and Aunt Florence suggested that I treat Erné to a movie for her birthday to celebrate the occasion. I did not appreciate being told what I should do and with whom, especially in front of her.

Not wishing to hurt her feelings, though, I took her anyway. I don't recall what movie we saw. But, I do remember that I kissed her good night before I descended the twelve steps to my basement quarters and she went to the bedroom she shared with Gisela on the main floor. I thought afterwards how convenient it was to have a girlfriend living in the same house. It saved on telephone bills and gasoline for the car. That was our second official date.

As time progressed, I became more aware of Erné's charm and beauty as well as her cheerful blue eyes while she sat across the table from me during family meals. I liked her captivating smile and the twinkle in her eyes. She began to blush when our eyes met. I looked forward to helping her with her English homework, too. I found myself thinking about her when I was at work and became aware that Erné might have a major effect on my future plans.

During the summer, Gisela and Erné obtained their drivers' permits expecting that Uncle Gene and I would teach them how to drive a car. They preferred me and my 1957 Plymouth Fury to Uncle Gene. This automobile had a revolutionary push button shift on the dashboard. Driving was easier because stick shifts and stick levers on the right side of the steering column were eliminated.

Weather permitting, we reserved Saturday afternoons for our "driver's training". We would drive along Delaware Ave. and Salem Church Rd. The sharp right hand turn up hill from Delaware Ave. on to Salem Church Rd. was tricky and the girls often killed the motor by not giving enough gas. I often heard, "Please don't take us around that horrid turn." Of course I enjoyed the look of terror in their eyes and rejoiced when they finally conquered the feat thereby displaying satisfaction while flashing million dollar smiles. Gisela remarked on several occasions that I criticized her driving more than Erné's after our outings.

Gisela took notice that my relationship to Erné was more affectionate than casual and that I was falling in love with Erné. She was happy about that and supportive of our courtship. Gradually our threesome dates to dances and church socials became twosome dates, as Erné and I needed time together to discuss our feelings toward one another and our future plans together. The more time we spent together, the deeper our love grew and the more we found we had in common. Erné insisted that she would not wait for me to finish my education before we got married. I realized that I needed to make a decision soon if I didn't want to lose her.

One fall Sunday afternoon, I requested a summit meeting among the five members in the Bulach home. I laid out my future plans and the options in front of me. I requested their input. It was quite a free for all, but very productive in the sense that everyone's opinion was heard and I was left to make the final call.

That same evening I decided to buy out Uncle Gene's business and plans were set in motion for his 1964 retirement. I would also spend my savings of $9,000, earmarked for education, toward the down payment of a new house. That home would be built on the empty lot adjoining Uncle Gene and Aunt Florence's property. This would also assure that I would be available to care for them in their old age.

The five of us agreed, also, that Erné and I should become engaged. I proposed to Erné a few months later on Christmas Day and we made plans to get married in our church on May 28, 1960. Requesting permission from Erné's parents for our marriage was a mere formality. They sensed from Erné's letters that the die was cast and our minds were made up. By that time, I assumed they knew that Erné was in good hands.

I contacted Fred Remmele regarding my decision. He was a gentleman, congratulated me on my choice and wished me good luck. He also left the door open should I choose to work for him in the winter months. It was very important to him to maintain his friendly relationship with Uncle Gene. Bulach Construction continued doing concrete work for Remmele Engineering on a contract basis for 60 years!

Erné and I asked Stan Bester to draw up plans for our new house. We hired Al Kamish's excavation business to dig the basement. Al emigrated from Czechoslovakia about the same time that Uncle Gene and Fred Remmele came over from Germany. The cost of the foundation excavation was $60. If Erné and I planned to move into our new home on our wedding day, we needed to get the basement in, the house enclosed and the roof on before winter set in. We could complete the inside during the winter months.

The footings for our home at 1259 MacArthur Ave. were poured and the basement walls laid-up during evening hours after work and weekends with the help of some co-workers, friends and Uncle Gene's supervision. Gretsfeldt Homebuilders completed our house by mid-April 1960 for $14,000. Adding in the cost for all concrete and masonry work, which I did largely on my own with the help of friends, the entire cost, including landscaping, was $16,800. The $9,000 I had saved up for my education was used to pay off half of the mortgage with the balance financed by Uncle Gene as a contract for deed at 4% interest.

After we paid for the appliances and hung shades and curtains, there was enough money left in the budget to purchase a complete bedroom set. A simple card table with 4 folding chairs became our dining room set. The rest of the house was void of any furniture. But it was a great start. It was, after all, our castle.

Our wedding day was glorious with beautiful sunshine and temperatures in the 70°F range. The wedding ceremony was conducted at St. Paul's Evangelical and Reformed Church, 900 Summit Ave., St. Paul, Minnesota (later renamed St. Paul's United Church of Christ) with

Rev. Erwin Koch conducting portions of it in German and Rev. Samuel Schmiechen finishing the last portion in English. Helmut Schwarz, my brother-in-law to be, was my best man and Gisela, my sister and Helmut's wife-to-be, was Erné's maid of honor. Cousin Ruth was the second attendant and Sally Lundgren was the flower girl.

Although our parents and other siblings were not present, the church was filled with approximately 200 guests; most were friends and distant relatives of Gene and Florence. There were many I didn't even know. Erné's Entgelmeier relatives, uncle, aunt and cousin, Harold, the other groomsman, represented her side of the family.

The reception (a sit down meal, open bar, and a wedding dance) was held in the Swift Union Hall in South St. Paul. The catering and hall rental cost for 200 guests was $600. The 3 man old-time band cost $80 and played from 9 p.m. until 1 a.m. Per city code, we had to vacate the Hall by 1:30 a.m. Aunt Florence's motto for this "once in a lifetime" occasion was ***"Man muss die Feste feiern, wie die Feste fallen."*** (We must celebrate important events as they come.)

The party continued for the younger crowd with the remaining cases of beer and left over food at our new house. Erné and I thanked and bid good-bye to our wedding guests and arrived home to a packed house. We could hardly get inside as it was wall-to-wall people. Luckily our bedroom was spared and only used for a repository of coats and purses.

Beer cases served as furniture to sit on. If you sat on a crate with some full bottles of beer left in them, you had to get up as soon as someone needed another beer. As I recall, the after party broke up after all the beer cases were completely dry and the schnapps and food had disappeared. Erné was almost in tears when she saw her new house a mess. It reeked of cigar and cigarette smoke, and there was food and beer spilled all over her new oak floors.

Fortunately, we had not planned to spend our wedding night at our new home as Gene and Florence suggested. We made reservations at the Lakes and Pines Motel on White Bear Ave. and Hudson Rd. (now a gas station). We arrived just as dawn was breaking, both totally exhausted. Uncle Gene reluctantly gave me two days off from our very busy schedule for the honeymoon. His advice to us was: "Save your money. Stay home. Lock the doors and pull the shades." We spent Sunday and Monday night at the Kaiserhof Hotel in New Ulm and visited the 'Hermann the German' monument.

We both wondered if it was divine guidance or coincidence that brought two young immigrants from the same German town together on a different continent 5,000 miles away. Six weeks later, Gisela and Helmut were married in Echterdingen, Germany. Gisela wore the same wedding dress Erné wore. They split the $38 cost of the dress.

Our early years of marriage flew by quickly and seemed, in some ways, like a dream. Erné and I were both busy. She set up and decorated our house, while I was working days and weekends for Uncle Gene. I had the regular work during the day and used the after hours time to follow up on leads and write job estimates. I am grateful to my Schatz, Erné, for her strength, patience and support.

Our son, Steven Mark, was born on September 4, 1961 at Bethesda Hospital in St. Paul. Erné very fittingly labored for 2 hours on Labor Day. I was among the expectant fathers in the waiting room eager for news of the Bulach ***Stammhalter*** (son and heir). Our second child, Kristina Jean, was born on Nov. 5, 1964. We rushed to the emergency room because delivery was imminent. I had barely registered Erné in at admissions when the phone rang and the nurse congratulated me on the arrival of a healthy baby girl.

In December 1965, we decided we could afford the $1,600 for round-trip airfare to Germany to visit our parents. I had not seen my parents in 11 years and Erné had not seen her parents in 8 years. Since we shut down our construction during the winter in those years, we decided to spend 3 months in Germany with our family. We wanted to meet our in-laws and show off our children. We also wanted to be home over the Christmas and New Year holidays to attend the baptism of the twins, Armin and Wolfgang Kehrer, to whom we were godparents. Uwe was already 5 years old and Rainer was 3 years old. Between the two families, there were six children, four of which were in diapers.[33] Tina began walking during that time and became quite attached to Erné's brother, Helmut. Helmut was the only person who could console Tina or get her to sleep when Erné and I couldn't.

We enjoyed a great deal of family time. Erné and I managed a 1-week second honeymoon trip to Innsbruck and Stenberg am Aachensee, Austria. We were the only hotel guests for four days at a regional hotel and enjoyed the romantic solitude of the area and the attentiveness of the hotel staff. Steve and I had a 1-day outing to the historic university town of Tübingen traveling via streetcar, bus and train. We saw the castle, city hall with the Count Eberhard mural on its façade and walked the Promenade along the Neckar River.

In 1962 Uncle Gene and Aunt Florence financed a trip from Stuttgart to St. Paul for my parents. My parents could then see firsthand how well Erné and I were adjusting to marriage and our new country. My father was eager to come, but my mother's fear of flying was greater than her curiosity of our new life. She had hardly been out of the state of Baden-Wuerttemberg and was most comfortable in her familiar surroundings.

Erné's mother, Erna, and my sister, Marianne, availed themselves of the opportunity instead. A highlight of their 4-week visit from mid-August to mid-September was a one-week road trip to Yellowstone National Park, Wyoming. At one of their picnic sites in a campground, a bear lumbered out of the bushes toward their food. The ladies were in a panic, but Uncle Gene charged the bear with a broken tree limb chasing it up a tree. The bear remained in his perch until the picnickers departed.

Erné and I, with 1-year-old Steve, took them for a week trip along the North Shore of Lake Superior in Minnesota to Gooseberry Falls then in to Canada to Port Arthur and Fort Williams (present day Thunder Bay). We continued west on the Trans-Canada Highway to Kakabeka Falls, Ontario and back to Minnesota via International Falls. Steve was not quite walking, yet refused to crawl on his knees on the grass. He walked on his hands and feet like a monkey. This still makes me chuckle when we watch our home movies.

It was emotionally difficult for our guests to return to Germany. Ludwig Erhard's Wirtschaftswunder was just getting off the ground and the gap in standard of living between Germany and the United States was great. They returned, however, with the satisfaction that Erné and I were well situated with family, housing and job security.

It was not until 1968 that my mother and father finally came to visit us in St. Paul. Mother finally decided to see what the magic was that held her son and meet her grandchildren, Steve and Tina.

My father was eager to see and learn all he could about this country during his 1-month stay. He had been anti-American due to his wartime experience, but gradually put aside his grudge. Father was impressed by the diversity, the wide-open spaces, the availability of building lots and the vastness of Lake Superior in comparison to Germany's Lake Constance. He returned again in 1970 with Gisela, Helmut and their daughters, Linda and Heike.

Erné's parents came to visit us in the fall of 1969. Mother Erna was familiar with the area from her previous visit. Father Friedrich felt he had reached paradise. He loved the sights around the Twin Cities and was appalled at the news coverage about the potential teardown of the Landmark Center in downtown St. Paul for the Rice Park redevelopment. His comment was this: "You Americans spend thousands of dollars to come to Europe to visit our castles and cathedrals and you have this magnificent building in your midst that you want to tear down? You should have your heads examined if you go through with that plan." Fortunately, this historic building was saved. When we weren't traveling with them, Friedrich would sew beautiful wool pantsuits for Erné and several items of clothing for the grandchildren.

We were happy that Erné's father was able to experience his daughter's life in the U.S. She was his ***Augapfel*** (apple of his eye). Sadly he died of heart failure only 2 1⁄2 months after he returned to Germany at the age of 58.

Erné and Tina returned to Germany for the funeral. They encountered some complications with passports because at that time Tina and Steve were on the same passport. She could leave the U.S., but could not reenter without her brother. Tina was able to have her own passport issued at the American Consulate in Munich thanks to our attorney and family friend, Rollin Crawford. He contacted U.S. Senator Hubert Humphrey in Washington D.C. and had the process expedited so that Erné's return flight to the U.S. was not delayed.

Steve traveled to Germany with the Laubach family in 1973 to stay with his Bulach and Kehrer relatives. He went again during our slow winter season after becoming a cement mason apprentice. He worked for his Uncle Fritz Elsasser in the German construction industry learning about methods and materials in the European market. Returning from this trip Steve asked, "Dad, how could you have left such a beautiful and great country like Germany?" I'm glad he didn't have to experience Germany during the devastating war years of WWII.

When Tina was in junior high school, she and I traveled to Germany together. We took a side trip to Garmisch-Partenkirchen, Zugspitze and Innsbruck. Tina inherited her mother's charming personality and quick smile, which contributed to her popularity at home and in Germany. The Kehrer cousins treated her like a princess and they all enjoyed the time they spent together.

Considering that we live almost 5,000 miles from our birthplace and from our closest relatives, Erné and I have excellent contact and relations between our families. Rarely do we miss one year without a trip to Germany or a visit from one of our siblings or an extended family member to our home in Minnesota. We are truly blessed by these very important connections.

Erné in Springtime

L-R: Helmut Schwarz, Gisela Bulach, Erné, Eberhard, Ruth Degler, Harold Entgelmeier, Sally Lundgren

Return to Germany 1955

Eberhard, Florence and Eugene Bulach - Hawaii 1958

CHAPTER 10

BUILDING A BUSINESS

"Von der Stirne heiss, rinnen muss der Schweiß, soll das Werk seinen Meister loben, doch der Segen kommt von oben!" ~ Friedrich Schiller

From the heated brow, sweat must freely flow, that the work may praise the Master, though the blessing comes from above.

Friedrich Schiller's poem ***Das Lied von der Glocke*** (Song of the Bell) has inspired me throughout my life. The poem compares the casting of a new bell at the foundry with the life of people within a community. The bell marks the milestones of life, its possibilities and its risks, with its pealing. Festive ringing announcing births and marriages of youth. Ticking away the passing years, announcing work and harvest. Proclaiming freedom through rebellion. Sending alarms with storms, then mourning death with the funeral toll. The product of your efforts in life (the bell) should be a credit to the blessings given by God (the creator/craftsman).

At the same time that Erné and I married, Uncle Gene and Aunt Florence purchased a farm near Stacy, Minnesota. Their vision was to turn this into a tree farm that would become their focus upon their retirement from construction. Many of my summer weekends were spent there with Uncle Gene underpinning the old farmhouse to build a basement that would accommodate a furnace, a hot water heater and additional storage. The kitchen was also completely remodeled and the house became livable year-round. This time away from my family was all donated labor.

Uncle Gene, on occasion, encouraged me by saying, "Some day, Eberhard, this will all be yours!" His 140 acres included an area for trees as well as a duck slough and some forest. In the fall we went duck hunting at daybreak until 9 a.m. and then worked the rest of the day on the farmhouse. In November we would deer hunt in these woods after returning from the annual deer hunting trip to Holyoke, Minnesota.

In addition to Uncle Gene's jobs for me, I also had 2 weeks of "summer camp" at Fort Ripley as a chaplain assistant with the Minnesota National Guard (Viking Division). This was a 2-year commitment to active reserve duty after completing my 2-year active duty obligation.

The transition from employee of Eugene Bulach Cement Contractor Co. to owner and operator of E.L.Bulach Construction Co. was merely a change of address and letterhead. Uncle Gene retired in the spring of 1964 as planned. By mutual agreement, I signed a promissory note for $5,000 to buy out his company. He charged me 4% interest and the note was to be paid off in

5 years. It was not difficult for me to assume the role of a business owner since I assumed most of the business responsibilities during the last two years of his and Aunt Florence's ownership. They wisely allowed me to assume responsibilities gradually in preparation for the position of sole ownership.

I was fortunate to have an established clientele as I got started in business. Uncle Gene became a volunteer consultant and promoted me whenever former clients called him. However, he did warn me not to get "big headed" after I bought a big new dump truck, which I had painted blue and added a new logo. He feared I would be unable to pay off his loan on time. I put his worries to rest by paying off his loan in 4 years. One year early!

During those four years, Erné was home with two young children, we paid off the business loan and the home mortgage, and we furnished our new home. We were on a tight budget. Without Erné's dedication, vision and expert money management, we would not have been able to pull it off.

As time went on, Uncle Gene's words of caution and frugality turned to words of praise. "You and your boys are doing good work." On several occasions, if he was in the area of one of our jobs, Uncle Gene would come by around 3 p.m. with a six-pack of beer saying, "Okay boys let's take a break." Uncle Gene's offer was never refused.

One day we drank our beer on the front steps of the church entrance we were working on. The pastor thought we were being disrespectful of the "House of God" and said so. Uncle Gene replied that the boys were taking early communion and they could leave and let the pastor finish the job.

The pastor shook his head, threw up his arms and walked away. When the church paid the bill, there was a handwritten note from the pastor saying, "Great job, boys!" There was no mention of the beer break.

I joined the Viking Toastmasters at the encouragement of Bill Sather, who was a concrete salesman for Certified Concrete Co., one of our material suppliers. As a business owner, I needed to develop public speaking and communication skills. I also took a Dale Carnegie course on "How to Stop Worrying and Start Living". These activities helped me immensely in my life as I dealt with customers and employees. My self-confidence improved, too. I am ever thankful to Bill for his recommendation.

In 1962 I joined the St. Paul Concrete and Masonry Contractors Association and the St. Paul Builders Exchange. I was asked to represent them on the soon to be formed Union Cement Masons Pension Fund as one of four employer members on the eight member Board of Trustees. I declined initially as it would take away more time from my family and work. However, I conceded and joined after learning how the Taft Hartley Pension Funds were being mismanaged. If I was obligated to pay in 5 cents per hour to the future pension of my hardworking employees, then I wanted to be sure that the money was going to be in their bank accounts upon their retirement.

I resigned as financial secretary of the Minnesota Cement Masons Pension Fund on November 20, 2006 after serving as a trustee for 40 years. I am proud of our accomplishments and investments when I see that a life long cement mason can expect to receive pension benefits on average of $3,500-4,000 per month from this fund, in addition to Social Security.

Looking back, I wonder where the hours came from for family responsibilities, active participation and contribution to volunteer organizations, and running a business. I always enjoyed the times when Steve and Tina brought their friends to our Deutscher Klub, Soccer Club and Volksfest Association dances to be part of the good ethnic food, refreshments and fun with our German friends. It was the way I could share my heritage with them and spend time together as they were growing up.

In business as in life, there are stages that mark progress and the fulfillment of dreams. I like to sit back and reflect on the monumental events in my business life and will relate them here.

When I took over Uncle Gene's construction business in 1964, he and I agreed that sooner, not later, I needed a new construction yard and a suitable building for office space, equipment warehousing and forming materials. Up until that point, Uncle Gene stored some of his equipment in his detached 3-car garage. Forms and related materials were on the three empty lots, which he purchased for $200, located across the alley behind his house. Those lots were part of a slough that extended from the alley to Kruse St. and further south that encompassed 6 city lots each 120 feet long and 40 feet wide. This land held water most of the year and was perfect duck, muskrat, rabbit and raccoon habitat.

Uncle Gene began filling the lots closest to his house with broken concrete, dirt and debris from his construction jobs. This fill soon amounted to enough ground that enabled him to use the area as his own construction yard. Such use wasn't permitted in a residential area, but the City turned a blind eye to this activity as long as the surrounding neighbors did not complain. As long as the neighbors were allowed to dump their own grass clippings, extra dirt, and other biodegradable items, there was no complaint. Care was taken, however, not to allow the dumping of garbage or tree branches or shrubs in the hole because it would not compact well. All broken concrete was pushed over the edge and covered with topsoil. They realized that the lots would eventually become building sites.

In 1966 we purchased 20 acres of land from the Harry Krech farm located south of Glassing Florist at 7500 Babcock Trail. The $5,000 seemed to be a lot of money then, but I needed another dumpsite and storage area soon because Uncle Gene's lots were filling up. The new property had several deep depressions suitable for clean fill such as broken concrete and dirt. It was perfect for our needs.

Six years later, Jim Lennon, who was in the commercial real estate business, alerted me of a 4.5 acre construction yard near Highway 110 and Oakdale Ave. being sold by Hurley Construction. They were going out of business. The property was zoned as agricultural land without water or sewer hookup. It did have access to electricity, however, which was a huge benefit. Since it was partially fenced in and had a metal storage building on it, it was grandfathered as a permitted use area in the event the area was ever rezoned. Jim and I formed the B&L Company in order to purchase the property. Jim was a silent partner. I sold the Krech farm property using the proceeds as down payment for the new site.

This became an incredibly fortunate move. I was able to store all of our equipment and most of our forms and materials under one roof and keep it all secure. Also, other contractors in our industry rented space in the large fenced-in areas for their own storage needs: Dell Dahn Construction, Serice Construction and Peter Schlagel Masonry. A large portion of the yard area was rented to a highway towing company that needed a fenced and secure area. An old existing chicken coop served as their 24-hour office. The extra rental income helped defray the costs of real estate taxes, assessment and mortgage.

Approximately four years later, MN-DOT (Minnesota Department of Transportation) was purchasing land along the Highway 110 corridor as expansion for the Highway 494 right of way. They bought about one acre along our south property line bordering Highway 110 for close to $55,000. This was almost enough to pay off the mortgage on the original 4-acre parcel.

Once the Highway 494 right of way and the Babcock Trail bridge over the freeway were completed, city utilities, curbs and gutters were installed along our north and east property lines. This enabled us to build our long envisioned office-warehouse complex.

By 1980 the E.L.Bulach Co. had outgrown the basement office of our home at 1259 MacArthur Ave., West St. Paul. The business volume had increased, there were more employees, another estimator needed to be hired and we required administrative staff. We moved the business to the Evergreen Industries Complex at 4921 Babcock Trail where there was ample office space and parking. It was also only one block away from our construction yard and future office building location.

In 1991 we were able to buy out Jim and Carmen Lennon's share of the partnership and dissolve the B&L Company. In 1994, after much planning, Erné and I formed Bulach Development in order to draw up plans and secure financing for our proposed office building. Our dreams were fulfilled when we were able to move into our new building at 1870 - 50th St. E, West St. Paul on September 25, 1995. This has been our business address ever since.

That was Phase I. We completed an office warehouse space in this newly zoned "light industrial" area at 1848 - 50th St. E. in 1997 and have enjoyed full occupancy since its construction.

It took 31 years of planning, persistence and a great deal of patience to realize the 1964 dream of owning our own office building.

An article that had significant impact on my business came in the monthly Concrete Construction Magazine in early 1971. The article described the virtues of Bomanite, a process of adding color to the surface of freshly poured concrete and imprinting a pattern to the pliable concrete surface. This, I thought, was a very positive development in the concrete industry to enhance the appearance of an otherwise unattractive gray concrete pavement. Concrete with its 2000-year-old formula of Portland cement (derivation of clay soil clinkers), sand and crushed stone and gravel was the industry's most durable and economical building material invented by man. It was biodegradable and made from raw materials common throughout all parts of the world.

I gave strong consideration to this Bomanite idea. I was in the curb and sidewalk business and curb machines were becoming quite popular. My competitors were buying curb machines at $40,000 a piece. I decided not to follow the crowd, but to distinguish my business in a new and different way. Against the advice of Uncle Gene and Erné, I arranged for a meeting with Dan Sieben of the Bomanite Corporation in Palo Alto, California.

Bomanite Corporation was promoting and selling franchise licenses to qualified contractors in various construction markets throughout the country. Dan mentioned that a representative from Jesco (the largest concrete and masonry contractor in the Twin Cities area at that time) had made arrangements to come to Palo Alto two weeks later. Dan agreed, however, to meet with me one week earlier.

After spending two days with Dan visiting and inspecting some Bomanite installations, I agreed to sign on the dotted line and purchase a franchise license covering the entire state of Minnesota and the five western counties of Wisconsin for the cost of $5,000. Final approval of the deal hinged on Dan's visit to Minnesota to inspect our operation, workmanship, dedication to detail and craftsmanship. He also required references from my bank and concrete supplier. He was impressed by the cleanliness of our trucks, equipment and workforce.

Erné's fabulous cooking must have also made a good impression on Dan, too, as he accepted the $5,000 check that made our agreement binding. As a side note, the Jesco representative, upon hearing that I got the Bomanite license first, offered me $10,000 for our license or the purchase of our entire company for a negotiated price. We declined the offer, of course!

The early years of business were quite lean with regard to income. Some of my employees earned more money than I did. Under union rules we were obligated to pay the labor wages first. The material costs and Bomanite royalty payments came next. There were times when Erné and I questioned whether we should even continue with the business. There were plenty of opportunities for me to take employment elsewhere, return to Remmele and even sell our business and its assets. Luckily, Erné and I weathered the storms. We believed in our work and in the future of colored and imprinted concrete.

Peter Nasvik, who was a third year apprentice and a dedicated worker for me, was also caught up in the enthusiasm for this new innovation with concrete. Tom

Becken, our concrete supplier representing Transit Mix, also believed in the new process and product. The three of us formed a separate company for the exclusive purpose of Bomanite installations. We had to pay a royalty to Bomanite for each square foot installed as protection of the franchise and the patent rights. We met on July 29, 1971 at Erné's and my home to form the new company called 'Concrete Design Specialties'.

To fund the new company, we agreed to invest $5,000 each as one-third equal partners. Peter Nasvik was president since I remained president of E.L.Bulach Construction Co., I was secretary/treasurer and Tom Becken was a silent partner. Peter flew to California the week after the papers were signed for a six-day training course. He became familiar with the Bomanite process as well as the additional work steps and skills involved in making this a durable and great looking product. He also purchased an initial set of stamping tools.

Initially E.L.Bulach would provide its work force on a 'contract labor' basis to the new company. Once the process gained popularity in the industry, the increased workload would warrant the hiring of more qualified cement mason technicians. There was always a 'doubting Thomas' in the local industry. We often heard, "This process would work great in the moderate climates of California, Arizona and Florida, but not in a cold climate like Minnesota with its freezing and thawing cycles." However, we carried out our plan.

Some of the early installations did not turn out as we had expected. Essentially we had waited too long before doing the imprinting and we had to rework at least three of the first ten installations. Gradually we developed the feel for timing in applying the color, troweling the surface and imprinting with the stamps.

As soon as Peter, Tom and I realized the potential job growth with our new product, we took on three more silent partners in order to generate more working capital. We hardly needed to look for investors. People came to us interested in investing. Tom Richardson and Roger Lingofeldt were in the related construction supply business. Rollin Crawford, the attorney who drew up the corporation agreement, was also eager to invest in our venture. He wasn't even in the construction industry, but he could see the potential in this revolutionary product.

After one season of trial and error, our founding team split up. Peter wanted a larger share in the company. Tom and I didn't want the momentum to come to a halt so I agreed to sell my shares back to the other stockholders on the condition that I could purchase a second Bomanite license for our original license area. They retained the name Concrete Design Specialties and E.L.Bulach Construction Co. became its competitor. This created some tense feelings between me and the other investors, who were my friends.

I knew that I would be successful with my own Bomanite license. I learned from Uncle Gene to do the best job possible and not to be satisfied with mediocrity. The crew of men I had were by industry standards the best. One in five men who worked for me became a long-term employee because of his skills and commitment to excellence. Others either quit or were let go because they did not share the company's goal of striving for perfection in each job. E.L.Bulach Construction Co. had a reputation for excellent work and providing great service.

For a period of time, the scuttlebutt within the industry was that Concrete Design Specialties would hire all of E.L.Bulach's rejects. Our companies co-existed for several years. We even joined forces on two different projects because of deadline and workforce demands.

Over the years, other competitors have entered the colored and imprinted concrete market. Within our franchise rights, the Bomanite process was patent protected, but the imprinting stamps were not. Anyone could copy and alter our patterns slightly and use them as they pleased. Ultimately, it came down to good workmanship and customer satisfaction. These two ingredients, combined with the Bomanite process, contributed to our success and many industry awards throughout the years.

In 2004 our son, Steve, completed the 10-year buy out of E.L.Bulach Construction Co. Not long after that, he was approached by the directors of Custom Rock (Concrete Design Specialties had evolved into Custom Rock) to negotiate a possible merger between the two companies. It made perfect sense to combine forces to gain a bigger market share while eliminating our most formidable competitor. The workforce would double and larger projects could be taken on not only in Minnesota, but in other parts of the United States as well. So, on January 1, 2006 E.L.Bulach Construction Co. merged with Custom Rock to form the new company Bulach Custom Rock.

I applauded and encouraged Steve's decision to spread his wings and take on more responsibility as the CEO of

Bulach Custom Rock. After one year of operation, the sales and profits were beyond expectation. I am very proud of the new management team and the employees.

"Someday, Mr. Bulach, I will work for you and be a worker just like you!" This statement was made by Jerome Furey our 7-year-old neighbor in a very serious tone with an equally serious look on his face. I automatically responded with, "Jerry, you will change your mind a hundred times by the time you graduate from high school." Jerry's profound statement was made on a Saturday morning when the two of us were returning from doing a cost estimate on a new job and making the final inspection from the previous week's work.

Our relationship began one Saturday morning when I was driving out of our driveway to start my usual rounds. I motioned to Jerry to move the beer can goal posts that were blocking my path. He asked me if he could come along for the ride. I told him yes, if he had his mother's permission. Wide-eyed he quickly ran home to get his mother's approval without concern that he was leaving his team without a goalie. He hopped in the truck and waved good-bye to his teammates saying, "I'm going to work with Mr. Bulach!" Two of his other teammates wanted to come, too, but I told them they needed to stay back or there wouldn't be enough people for two hockey teams.

Early on, Jerry wasn't too interested in working and getting his clothes and hands dirty. He was happy to ride in the truck with me. The pickup ride on Saturday mornings was the highlight of his week. It was more exciting even than playing street hockey or kickball with the near thirty neighborhood children.

Jerry was always full of excitement and eager to help. As a child he was somewhat underfoot, but he was good company and a talkative companion. To his credit he never became discouraged. Before long he learned how to handle a tape measure by himself and push an empty wheelbarrow without tipping it over. When our rounds lasted longer than three or four hours, we stopped at McDonald's for refreshment. I allowed him to order whatever he wished on the menu as long as he ate it all. He never wasted a bite following his boss' example. Once in a while I gave him some loose change for his piggy bank, which was like a "bonus" for him.

I purchased a pair of Red Wing work boots for me and inquired about children's sizes. In that "tennis shoe generation" there wasn't much need for children's work boots. I special ordered a pair for Jerry that cost nearly as much as my own adult pair. He wore those work boots with great pride. He wore them to church, to school and even to play street hockey because he was a "worker". Jerry's mother even oiled his boots periodically, "just like Mr. Bulach."

One Saturday morning Erné woke me up around 7:15 saying, "There is something or somebody banging at our back door. It sounds like grating metal. You better go check it out." I found Jerry sitting on the step eating the lunch that his mother had packed for him. He thought we started work at 7:00 a.m. instead of 8:00 a.m. as I had told him. He was eager to get on with the day and was bored waiting so he decided to eat his lunch, that way he would have that over with and he could work without interruption. Jerry also knew that he would never go hungry while working with me.

Jerry's and my routine continued for several years and soon included summers. When Steve, who was four years younger than Jerry, got old enough, he joined our crew. Steve came along initially for the truck ride, lunch at McDonalds and other perks, and, eventually, a pair of work boots of his own. Jerry took Steve under his wing and became a role model. Jerry was always punctual waiting for us at the back steps. He was suddenly the expert in all areas and instructed his tutee on how to hold a broom and read a tape measure. It was hilarious at times watching and listening to the interaction of the two boys.

Whenever conversations turned to life goals and future jobs, Jerry never wavered from his little boy dream. Following his high school graduation, Jerry became a cement mason apprentice while working simultaneously for E.L.Bulach. His previous years of "on the job training" gave him a leg up in his apprenticeship class at the vo-tech. He finished his apprenticeship in 3 1⁄2 years and became the best 'step man' in the entire Twin Cities Masons Local #553. I believe he and his crew could out perform any other crew in workmanship, productivity and overall performance.

Jerry did indeed fulfill his dream. Jerry became a job superintendent and estimator for Bulach Custom Rock. I am convinced that it is Jerry's early example and leadership that encouraged Steve to become a construction worker like his father. To have my son follow in my footsteps and take over the family business is truly a wonderful gift.

❖

The notion of after work "Happy Hour" began spontaneously one hot Friday afternoon in 1972. The tradition has continued for more than 46 years as a way to maintain friendships and open dialogue between employer and employee.

Happy Hour's intent was to thank Bulach Construction employees for their hard work at the end of a busy and strenuous work week. To reward a "job well done" and satisfy exhausted workers' thirst, I offered each employee up to two beers before they left the shop. The reason was to get the men home with a full paycheck without stopping by the bars first. I learned many years later that this practice was greatly appreciated by many spouses.

Back in 1964 when E.L.Bulach Construction was started, employees were paid in cash, a common practice of the day. Pay Envelopes were filled with the week's wages. The money was taken out at home and the envelope was returned to the company in time for the next week's payday. A problem developed when payroll checks were issued instead of cash envelops.

Employees were paid at the end of the day Friday and families would have to wait until the following week Monday to cash or deposit their paychecks because banks were closed on Saturday and Sunday. The bars were the easiest place to cash a check sooner. This presented a problem in some households. When the husband stopped by a bar on his way home from work. The check was cashed and an alcoholic drink was consumed. Temptation for excessive drinking was present and resulted in "lost" wages and a reduced paycheck arriving home.

Those early Happy Hours were composed exclusively of men. They became jam sessions and locker room conversations about sports, women, sex, the day's work, customers and even the boss. The informal atmosphere "lifted the tongues" of some of the quieter individuals who were too timid to speak up when something stuck in their "craw". Sometimes our lively and informative discussions included pro/con suggestions about the boss or our leadership!! It is always a learning experience when the boss hears the workers' perspective about a work situation.

After our office building was completed in 1995, Happy Hour re-located to the lower level shop and then to my office upstairs on the main floor. The location was season and weather dependent. Over the years, these sessions changed in scope and participants as Happy Hour no longer was limited to employees.

Over time, our building tenants and their employees found the Happy Hour gatherings entertaining and joined in to celebrate another successful week. Word spread. Members of our church, the Minnesota Builders Exchange, the St. Paul Club and family friends became frequent, if not regular, attendees. Some Fridays there was standing room only in the office. Guests began providing snacks to go along with the free beer. And, to my knowledge, I never suffered the embarrassment of running out of beer.

Eberhard starting out at Eugene Bulach Cement Contractor

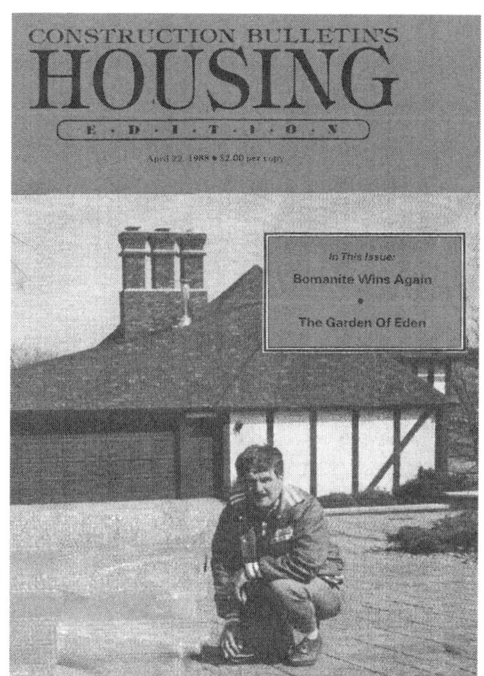

CONSTRUCTION BULLETIN'S

HOUSING

E · D · I · T · I · O · N

April 22, 1988 • $2.00 per copy

In This Issue:

Bomanite Wins Again

•

The Garden Of Eden

Construction Business

Bulach Custom Rock
L-R: Jim Turitto, Steve Bulach, Eberhard Bulach, Emily Erickson, Jerry Furey

50 Year Celebration

CHAPTER 11

LED BY FAITH

"To everything there is a season, and a time for every purpose under Heaven;
A time to be born, and a time to die:
A time to plant, and a time to pluck up what is planted;
A time to kill, and a time to heal;
A time to break down, and a time to build up;
A time to weep, and a time to laugh;
A time to mourn, and a time to dance;
A time to cast away stones, and a time to gather stones together;
A time to embrace, and a time to refrain from embracing;
A time to get, and a time to lose;
A time to keep, and a time to cast away;
A time to rend, and a time to sew;
A time to keep silence, and a time to speak;
A time to love, and a time to hate;
A time of war, and a time of peace."

~ Ecclesiastes 3:1-8

Certain sounds and smells during our lives leave lasting impressions. For me they include: my parents' voices, voices of siblings and playmates, bird sounds, ear splitting thunder cracks, loud fireworks and detonating bombs in a war zone. One of the most enduring and endearing sounds, however, is the pealing of the church bells in Echterdingen.

We didn't need wristwatches as children to tell time because the sounding of the vesper bells signaled that it was time to come home for dinner. The farmers in the field, per age-old custom, said a quick prayer for the day and headed home for dinner and additional chores.

The bell tower of our church is very tall and prominent. There are four bells of different sizes and a large clock face on three sides. The clock can be seen one kilometer away. The clock sounds every quarter hour starting with one bell on the quarter hour, two bells on the half hour and three bells on the three quarter hour. Four bells rang on the full hour followed by a deeper and louder sounding bell that chimed the indicated hour.

For example, four bell chimes followed by one low bell toll indicated 1:00; two low bell tolls indicated 2:00; and so forth. As children, we could never use the excuse that we didn't know the time because we could hear the bell chimes at least 2 km away depending on the direction of the wind.

The church bells rang every morning at 6:00 a.m. during weekdays in summer and in winter. During the winter, the bells were rung at night at 6:00 p.m. and 8:00 p.m. when it was dark. The quarter hour continued throughout the day and night. On Sundays and religious holidays, the four bells began ringing at 8:30 a.m. for five minutes. At 9:00 a.m. two bells would ring to remind parishioners that they had one half hour until the worship service began. At 9:25 a.m. all the church bells would ring for 5 minutes, stopping promptly at 9:30 am. The pastor would stand up from his seat at the chancel and the organist would begin playing the prelude. The vespers bell would sound again during the saying of the Lord's Prayer.

At 11:00 a.m. the bells would chime again to signal the coming of the midday meal at noon. The smallest and highest pitched bell rung alone indicated that someone in the town had died. The ringing of two bells meant that a burial would take place in 30 minutes. The ringing of three bells or all of them together meant that a wedding ceremony would take place in 30 minutes.

The ringing of the vespers bell corresponded with the seasons. There was no set time for this ringing except at dusk. This bell indicated the end of the workday: children were to go home, farmers were to come in from the field and laborers were to stop their work. The night bell rang at 8:00 p.m. daily to indicate bedtime. In the olden days, the bells rang in emergency situations such as a fire in the town or the approach of enemy troops during war.

The bells would have rung loud and long on May 8, 1945. However, all of the large bells, except the "death" bell, were taken out of the bell tower in 1943 and melted down into gun barrels for the war effort. The missing bells were replaced during the early 1950s as bronze material became available again and donations from parishioners could pay for new bells.

Each time I return to Echterdingen to visit, I practically fall out of bed the first morning that I am there. We stay in the home of my brother-in-law, Helmut and Margot Kehrer, which is only one block away from the church. The bells are so loud they sound like they are right outside my window.

Parents with small children, retirees and people working late shifts have complained about the 6 a.m. and 8 p.m. church bells. However, the majority of Echterdingen's citizens don't want to do away with this centuries-old tradition.

After 3-4 days I sleep right through them and the airplanes from the Stuttgart airport again. Even at our home in Sunfish Lake, MN, the airplane noise gets blocked out of our minds.

When I hear the familiar sounds of the church bells, I become quite sentimental. These bells were an integral part of my growing up years in Germany. They rang in happy and sad times. The memories they generate for me are mostly happy ones and I feel as though they say "Welcome Home!" when I return.

The word "mother-in-law" often has negative connotations and bears the brunt of crazy jokes. For me, however, any negative association is completely unjustified. My mother-in-law was a gem. Erna Kehrer was born on January 30, 1914 in Mannheim. She spent most of her life in Echterdingen.

I met Erna Kehrer sometime during the terrible war years of 1939-1945. She was a sales clerk at the only milk store in town. My mother sent me there to purchase our family's daily milk ration as soon as I was big enough to carry the 2-liter milk container.

As many as four saleswomen were behind the dairy counter pouring milk into customer provided containers each day. I always lined up behind the counter position of Erna Kehrer because she always had a pleasant smile and a kind word for everyone in spite of the difficult conditions we were living under. The seemingly endless months and years of hunger and uncertainty during the war was visible in the faces of all the people and influenced their behavior. People became almost like zombies. People became calloused to other people's feelings.

My dear mother and Erna Kehrer were notable exceptions to me. Erna's friendly and sincere smile was just like a welcome ray of sunshine after a full day of rain. I never dreamed that this kind person, who I adored as a child, would one day become my mother-in-law. When I first met Erna Kehrer, her daughter Erné was only 4 years old. Once I left for the United States, I didn't see Erna Kehrer again until 1964 as my mother-in-law.

Since we knew each other, we hit it off instantly. We had a mutual respect for one another and there was never an unkind word spoken between us. The fact that she visited us in St. Paul at least 14 times, the last time in 1998 at age 84, indicates the love and respect we had for one another. She felt at home with us and she was always a welcome guest in the homes our friends as well. She was loved and admired for the kind person she always was.

During one of my visits to Germany in the 1970s to visit my ailing mother, I was invited to be a groomsman in Ursula Dorn's sister's wedding in Klingenberg near Heilbron. Erika married Tony Geiger and I was asked to escort their other sister, Lore, at the ceremony. Since Erné was back home with the children, the bride's family wanted me to bring one of my sisters as a guest. Since both of my sisters were unable to join me due to other commitments, I asked my mother-in-law, Erna, to be my date. It certainly surprised a few people, but we had a great time and even danced a few times. Everyone enjoyed Erné's mother!

Erna was the last ***Oma*** (grandmother) in our own family as well as in our friendship circle. She passed away on July 8, 2005. She is sorely missed, but we all have fond memories of her life with us. She was truly an angel on earth. I say, rest in peace, you good and faithful servant of God.

Ecclesiastes 3:1-8 (KJV) in the Bible, I find befits my mother-in-law, Erna Kehrer, because of her positive attitude and ability to make the best of every situation in life, believing that everything had its time and place.

I reflect often about my beginnings in the United States and the faith community that surrounded me. As I journeyed to St. Paul, I felt like one of the three wise men following the star to Bethlehem. While the wise men traveled in search of the Christ child, I was traveling in search of my promised land. I was leaving a ragged, war-torn Europe in search of opportunity and a better life, just like millions of other immigrants who came before me.

The friendly reception by the members of St. Paul's Evangelical and Reformed Church helped me immensely in my assimilation to the American culture. It was not popular at that time to be of German descent and my accent gave away my origins. The St. Paul's community became my ***Ersatz*** (substitute) family along with Uncle Gene, Aunt Florence and Cousin Ruth.

Because 90% of the congregation was of German heritage, I was welcomed with open arms. I had a place that sheltered me from the hatred and disparaging remarks I received in public: "Where do you come from?" "You must have been a Nazi."

People were extremely helpful and concerned that I felt at home among them; every day, not just on Sunday mornings. They spoke German with me at times, I was offered clothing, I was invited to social outings and I was even offered rides to church activities because I could not drive.

The congregation moved from the St. Paul Capitol approach area on Tilton St. to a newly built church building at 900 Summit Avenue in May 1952. I was among a group of 50 people in the first membership class at this new location.

Erné and I were married at St. Paul's. Steve and Tina were baptized, confirmed and married there. We have all participated actively in many different groups and projects over the years. Erné led the women's group in their annual fruitcake baking and sale, the Oktoberfest choir fundraising dinner and many other forms of hospitality. I have served on the Building and Grounds Committee, the Church Council and the Childhood Center Board.

This faith community, now called St. Paul's United Church of Christ, has been my anchor, my home and my family. How fortunate I am to be part of this community of Christians who truly care for one another in sickness and in health, from cradle to grave. I have been blessed beyond measure.

The aphorism "There are no atheists in foxholes" can be heard at times of extreme stress or fear, often in conjunction with military combat when soldiers cry out to a higher power to save them from imminent death and destruction. However, I truly believe in the power of prayer at all times in my life because I know that it is God's grace that has spared me from death and defeat on several occasions in my life.

I have never been in a foxhole with live ammunition whizzing over my head, but a muddy roadside ditch did offer me concealment and protection from a strafing P-47 fighter plane. A fruit cellar also offered me security from high-flying bombers.

Though the stressful times in life give rise to crying and screaming to God for relief and preservation, it is truly the quiet moments where the promises of the Lord's Prayer speak to me and provide me comfort. I felt this in

2001 at the Mayo Clinic when the hospital chaplain came to my room early in the morning before my spinal cord surgery.

The chaplain offered to pray with me before the operation. I accepted. While his exact words escape me, he did ask God to give the surgeon patience and a steady hand in the delicate surgery he was about to perform. He also prayed that I would have peace and a positive attitude while undergoing the procedure. We both knew that the slightest false move could make me a paraplegic. I felt uplifted and confident, assured that all would be well.

Dr. Marsh, the neurosurgeon, entered the operating room, introduced himself and explained the procedure and its difficulty. He then asked me if I was ready for "a long nap". I assured him that I was ready and trusted his skilled hands.

In the end, all went well. I regained my ability to walk without support defying medical odds (United Hospital, St. Paul gave a 10% chance; Mayo Clinic, Rochester gave a 75% chance). My prayers were answered and I am truly grateful.

Goldene Hochzeit

50th Wedding Anniversary

2010

Eberhard and Erné

Eberhard, Erné, Gisela & Helmut Schwarz

Bulach and Schwarz

Steve, Erné, Eberhard, Tina

Erné with brother, Helmut Kehrer; Erna Kehrer, mother

12

REFLECTING ON LIFE

"Im Wein ist Weisheit, im Bier ist Kraft und im Wasser sind Bakterien!"

In wine there is wisdom, in beer there is strength and in water there is bacteria!
~ altered version of Benjamin Franklin's quote[34]

By dictionary definition, LIBERTY has many meanings. It is the state of being free within society from oppressive restrictions imposed by authority on one's way of life, behavior or political views. It is a right or privilege, especially a statutory one. It is the state of not being imprisoned or enslaved. It is the personification of liberty as a female figure. It is the power or scope to act as one pleases. It is a person's freedom from control by fate or necessity. In the nautical sense, it is shore leave granted to a sailor. Synonyms for this word and concept are privilege, immunity, license, right, exemption, right and free speech.[35]

The current world is full of individuals expecting and demanding the liberties listed above while simultaneously denying these same privileges to other nationalities, races and persons of differing political or religious persuasions. I find recent immigrants to the United States to be coddled by a social welfare system that hinders their personal growth and motivation. Upon arrival to this country they gain immediate access to Public Assistance Programs with interpreters brokering their needs. Unlike previous generations from around the world who were not pampered in this way.

Earlier generations of immigrants had the incentive to conform and find a job in order to survive. Hardship, disappointment and discrimination are all a part of life and should be expected. I learned at a young age that hard work pays off economically and socially. I came to the land of opportunity to avail myself of that opportunity – the results are evident!

Just as freedom is not free, liberty comes with a price. Every action or inaction has a consequence and no one lives immune to consequences. Entitlements must even be earned through some form of work or employment. The fact is, in life, there is no free ride. Why should the sweat of the “doers” in society bear the load for the “slackers”?

Voting in municipal, state and federal elections determine our city, state and country’s policy and compass heading. I believe that voting is a citizen’s privilege in a democratic society such as ours and should not be taken for granted.

What transpired the night of October 11, 1951 at 11 p.m. as I stepped off the ship at the American Lines shipping dock along the East River in New York City was indeed like re-birth. As we passengers sailed past the illumined Statue of Liberty, we looked straight ahead at Manhattan Island lit up in the distance like a Christmas display with the tallest structure in the center – the Empire State Building (the tallest Building in the world at that time) as the Christmas tree.

Welcome to the New World! And, what a world it was! Everything was bigger, better and more colorful in an unfamiliar, but futuristic, way. I was dead tired and worn out from the stormy 11 day voyage and looking forward to a good night of rest in a bed that did not move and sway constantly. All of a sudden, I was too excited to be tired. This must be what heaven is like, I thought to myself. I felt like hugging and kissing every person I met as I was overcome with sheer joy after disembarking from the ship. The fact that most of the people I encountered were of different ethnicities and spoke different languages did not bother me. They were my friends, fellow residents in "paradise".

I was shaking with excitement and drunk with emotion. In fact I was afraid to go to sleep out of fear that when I woke up this would all be a dream. Every breath I took, every minute that passed presented me with new surprises. I eagerly absorbed each experience like a thirsty person enjoying the first swallow of life giving water. Never in my wildest dreams did I envision that this is what America would be like. My companion, Richard Hess, could sense my enormous delight and complete awe of what I was witnessing. This gave him incentive to show me more surprises as we walked around New York City.

While I was living WW II in Europe, the Pacific theater was experiencing its own ravages. Years later, my connection to both wars collided during the 1970s when the E.L.Bulach Construction Company was asked to install a concrete base pad for the number-three 4"/50 caliber gun from the USS Ward. The gun had been installed as a memorial at the Minnesota State Capitol in St. Paul during the Minnesota Centennial celebration in 1958, but needed a new base. The gun was removed from the ship when it was converted to a high-speed transport and given to honor the men, Minnesota Naval Reservists, who fired it on December 7, 1941.

The USS Ward was a destroyer in Hawaii's Pearl Harbor that fired the first shot at a 2-man Japanese mini-submarine before the actual bombing. The ship was operating on local patrol duties in Hawaiian waters when on the morning of December 7, the ship's crew caught sight of a submarine periscope following a freighter through the entrance of the Pearl Harbor ships' canal.

The crew fired warning shots and eventually shot at the conning tower when the submarine did not communicate its advance. The submarine sank and the crew notified their commanding officers. Their radio communication failed to prompt an alert and no one believed the crew's reports for years after. The air attack on the harbor occurred 75 minutes later. It wasn't until

2002 that the crew of the USS Ward was vindicated when the submarine's wreckage was discovered on the ocean floor by the Hawai'i Undersea Research Laboratory.[36]

I still like to drive by the capitol approach by the gun on my way home from church because I am reminded of excellent concrete work that withstands time and weather. I remember my military service in Hawaii. And, I recall my own war experiences in Europe. In 2005 Erné and I visited Pearl Harbor with Helmut and Margot Kehrer. Visiting the Arizona and the battleship Missouri anchored across the bay, I noticed tears running down Helumt's cheek. He, too, felt the weight an emotion of historical change in both Europe and in the Pacific Islands.

Most people who were of grade school age or older on November 22, 1963 can remember the infamous day that impacted our "American way of life" forever; the day United States President John Fitzgerald Kennedy was assassinated. I remember that day well because I was in Canada on a hunting trip.

For several years, Russ and Buck Chaput, Uncle Gene and I went on an annual trip to Torch River, Saskatchewan, Canada to hunt moose. Torch River is 500 miles north of the U.S. border and was the last outpost of civilization before the "bush", as the locals called it. It was the end of the line and no gravel or paved roads went further north. We drove the distance in a pickup truck stopping only to refuel and change drivers every four hours.

Russ was our organizer and hunting guide. He had purchased the necessary aerial maps of the area in order to orient ourselves in the wilderness of virgin forests, lakes, streams and swamps known for its abundant animal habitat: moose, deer, wolf, coyote, lynx, fox beaver, rabbit, muskrat. Russ, Buck and Gene lived in a pickup mounted camper when hunting the year before. A "bush" farmer offered his log home if they returned; a nice amenity since there was snow and zero degree temperatures by that time of the year. The log house did not have indoor plumbing, but neither did the pickup camper. The cabin was kept warm and they provided our meals. There was a side room about as big as the cabin itself that stored the firewood.

Around lunchtime on November 22, we were warming ourselves around a campfire and eating our toasted sandwiches when the farmer came out to us on his 4-wheeler. He was clearly agitated and crying. He shouted, "Your president was shot in Dallas. President Kennedy is dead."

We were all stunned by the tragic news. How could such a thing happen to this very popular and energetic leader of our country? I was touched by the farmer's show of emotion and the tears he shed for our president. Such was John F. Kennedy's legacy. He was loved and respected by people around the world.

The early sixties was a time of incredible promise and growth for this great country of ours in technology, economics, and opportunity. Although we were at the height of the "cold war" with the Soviet bloc countries, especially due to the Cuban missile crisis, the "good life" was available anywhere throughout the country. To think that our president could be assassinated was beyond comprehension. The country's euphoric and invincible feelings were suddenly shattered. If our president wasn't safe, who was?

Kennedy was popular both nationally and internationally. He was charismatic, yet controversial. He showed promise of greatness, which was never fulfilled. Kennedy's beautiful and intelligent wife, Jacqueline aka Jackie, certainly captured everyone's attention as well. Jackie delivered speeches in French and Italian when visiting France and Italy, and was admired by the foreign press.

The United States has four in-office presidential assassinations: Abraham Lincoln, James A. Garfield, William McKinley and John F. Kennedy. President Lincoln's death caused great turmoil. President Garfield was assassinated four months into his term of office, but caused no great upheaval in the country's psyche. History books tell us that William McKinley was a popular president. His administration made the transition from the 19th to the 20th century. His assassination at the beginning of his second term in office must have jarred the country's citizenry. However, the same impression of greatness bestowed to Lincoln and Kennedy is not reflected in the minds of the average American.

We discussed amongst each other in our hunting party if we needed to break up the hunting trip and head home. We had just arrived and had plans for a 10-day hunt as stated on our 'alien hunting permits'. We wondered if the U.S. would close its borders and we would be stuck in

Canada for a while. After contemplating and weighing our options, we decided to stay the full term.

Whether by luck or hunting expertise, we filled our quota of 2 moose and 2 deer within two days. Since we could no longer hunt, we decided to assist the farmer by pouring a concrete floor for him in his hog barn. The farmer had purchased 24 bags of Portland cement and had sand and gravel delivered to his barn. He was surprised by the early winter and thought he would wait to complete the project in the spring. Uncle Gene and I knew that damp and cold weather would hydrate the cement making it useless by spring so we decided to give him a hand. The farmer was delighted with the plan.

The sand and gravel were frozen and we needed hot water to mix the ingredients in the 1/8 cubic yard mixer. Using Yankee ingenuity, we figured out a way to get the job done. We formed a regular production line. The two women heated all the water in the house on the wood stove. Jimmy, the 18-year-old son, brought cold water from the well to the house and brought the heated water to the mixer outside as soon as Russ and Buck had thawed enough sand and gravel for one batch. The water was mixed with 1 bag (90 lbs.) of cement. Uncle Gene operated the mixer and counted the ingredients of 9 shovels sand and 12 shovels gravel to 1 bag Portland then enough hot water to make the mixture workable and able to flow.

I took the wheel barrel full of concrete and dumped it in the designated area while the next batch was being mixed. We worked up a sweat even in the zero degree temperatures. To prevent the freshly poured concrete from freezing, we enclosed the area with tarps and plastic sheeting. We heated it as well with an electric salamander (space heater). The task was completed in two days, mixing a total of 24 batches of concrete. Under normal conditions, the project would have taken two to three men no more than one 8-hour day to complete.

The farmer was dubious of the results due to the adverse conditions, but was delighted with the near perfect job. We were pleasantly surprised to find the floor in good condition the following fall when we returned to Torch River for another hunting trip. A severe drought and poor harvest the next summer yielded less income, which would have made it impossible for the farmer to buy 24 more sacks of Portland cement.

Crossing the U.S. border in North Dakota on our return trip one week after Kennedy's assassination was a bit of a problem, not because of the political situation, but because we decided to cross at 2:00 in the morning. We wanted to beat the traffic at this border crossing. When we arrived, the border patrol agent was on his break and refused to respond to his ringing doorbell though he could see us through the window. The four of us were impatient and not interested in waiting so Uncle Gene pounded on the door. The agent warned us, "If you break the door, I will put you all in jail. I will be with you after I go to the bathroom."

We had aggravated the agent enough that he took his time with a thorough search of all of our bags. We had declared all of our Canadian purchases such as Canadian Club Whisky, sausage, bread and jam, plus we had proof of our hunting permits. Had there been a problem with that, he could have detained us at the border for a longer time. The four of us were angry at the agent's indifference and our travel delay. We lost two hours of driving time, but did make it home.

The hunting trips to Canada were quite fun while they lasted. Regulation from Canadian authorities became more stringent and Erné became less enamored with eating wild game so I resigned my palate to the much cheaper and less dangerous meats of pork, beef and chicken from the grocery butcher shop.

Canadian authorities began requiring local guides with "alien" hunters. It was questionable whether the locals knew any more than those of us who had been scouting and hunting the land for many years prior to the new law. Such was our experience in 1965.

Jim, a friend of our host's son, joined our hunting party on a particularly snowy day. We asked him if he had a compass in the event that he got lost in the woods. He responded, "I know this area like the back of my hand. I have been logging these woods for several years." He saw no need to take a compass. However, we should have insisted that he take one.

This young man shot and wounded a moose. He followed the drops of blood, continuing in pursuit of the animal well into the swamp. His shots had chased the moose away. He eventually ran out of ammunition and became completely disoriented and unable to follow his own tracks because of the falling snow. As it grew dark, he decided to camp under a tamarack tree with dry branches to start a small fire to warm himself. The young hunter's feet and socks had become soaking wet while tramping through the swamp. To his dismay, the matches in his breast pocket had become wet from his perspiration and he had no way to light the fire. He had to keep walking to prevent death by freezing or exposure.

In the meantime, the rest of the hunting party assembled at the meeting point prior to dusk. We realized that our young hunter was missing somewhere in the woods. We had heard Jim's shots in the woods, but could not determine his location or distance. As night descended, fanning out into the bush and swamps was a foolhardy option. We decided to make a bonfire leaving two men at this location. The farmer's son brought blankets, food and coffee from home understanding that we would stay in the woods until we found our missing party member. Uncle Gene and I walked along an abandoned logging trail to establish another lookout post and bonfire 3⁄4 mile away.

Periodically, we fired three quick shots in succession to announce our location. A lost person is expected to respond with one round of shot. This is a rule for hunting in the woods. There was no response. We kept our all night vigil in -10°F weather, taking turns walking between the bonfires to keep ourselves warm and awake until daybreak. We were all concerned that we might not find our friend alive in the morning.

Shortly after dawn as we prepared our new search, a jeep drove to our location with information that another hunting party had come across our lost companion on a logging road 5 miles away. He was soaking wet, shivering and incoherent. His feet were also frozen to his socks and boots. They drove him to the nearest healthcare clinic where he was hospitalized and lucky to be alive. His irresponsibility cost him two toes on one foot and a complete heel on the other. He had kept moving all night and eating snow to keep from dehydrating. Jim had heard our shots, but could not respond because he had run out of ammunition.

Jim learned a hard lesson that night and would be reminded of it every day of his life. I also learned a life lesson as well: never go hunting in the woods without a compass, dry matches and enough ammunition.

In March 1981 while I was in Germany, unfortunately without Erné and the children, my siblings invited me on a long weekend trip to Berlin. I had never been there and they knew that I would be interested in visiting the divided former capitol city of the Third Reich. There were six of us total: Marianne, her husband Fritz, Gisela, her husband Helmut, Fritz Jr. and me. The flight and hotel reservations were all pre-arranged. We decided on our daily itinerary once we landed in Berlin.

One day we visited East Berlin, which was in the Russian Zone. We crossed the border from West Berlin into East Berlin at 'Checkpoint Charlie'. To enter, each visitor was required to exchange 20 Deutsche Mark (DM) for 20 East German Marks, even though the eastern currency was worth only 1/5 the value of the western currency. It was illegal for merchants in the east to accept western DM. However, there was a black market exchange rate of 3 East German Marks to 1 West German DM. Visitors crossing into the East also paid 5 DM for a 1-day tourist visa.

Checkpoint Charlie had one gate for German citizens and another gate for foreigner tourists. A long line formed at the gate for East and West Germans, but there was no line for the other nationalities. I thought that I would be lucky and pass through the control faster in my line than my siblings in theirs. How wrong I was!

I entered a room with bare walls and a badly worn wooden floor. It was about 15 ft. square with only two doors, the one I had entered and the one I hoped to exit. On one wall was a counter with a glassed window 12" high and 48" wide above it at eye level. I pushed my American passport through the slot expecting to be waived on through after answering one or two questions regarding my intended visit. I saw two sets of eyes staring intently at me. A guard told me in perfect English to "have a seat". I sat in one of the two straight-backed chairs and waited. There were no windows or magazines, just drab walls full of smudges in desperate need of paint. After a 15-minute wait I went to the opening and asked the guard in German, ***"Haben Sie ein Problem mit meinem Pass?"*** (Do you have a problem with my passport?) Though he wore a Russian soldier's uniform, he responded in perfect German. ***"Nein, es dauert nur noch einige Minuten."*** (No, it will only take a few more minutes.)

My patience was tested another 15 minutes. I started to get nervous and I approached the counter again and asked how much longer it would take. Just one more minute was his answer. Finally another man appeared with my passport in his hand and asked how long I was staying in East Berlin and what location I was planning to visit. I also had to show him my 20 East German Marks. Without any apology for my delay, he handed me my passport and wished me ***"Schönen Aufenthalt"***. (Enjoy your stay.)

My siblings were extremely worried when I hadn't appeared from the border control. It had taken them only 15 minutes to pass through the very busy checkpoint. I was the only foreign visitor in my line and it had taken 45 minutes to go through the checkpoint.

We planned to visit some of the famous sites of the German Democratic Republic (***Deutsche Demokratische Republik*** - DDR). Our first impression was the empty streets. There were no cars, only a few pedestrians and a bicycle now and then. All the buildings were a drab and depressing gray and brown color. No window boxes or flowers decorated the properties either. There was visible damage to the exterior stucco and brick from bullets and grenades. It was 36 years since the end of WWII and no repairs had been done.

In West Berlin, the sidewalks were bustling with well-dressed pedestrians and shoppers, and the streets were full of Daimlers, Audis and BMWs, both cars and delivery trucks. Window boxes full of flowers and colorful shutters decorated the building facades. Neon signs were everywhere drawing attention to businesses and stores.

Our first stop was the Brandenburg Gate, Berlin's most famous landmark. The archway over the street was fenced in at that time for repair. Still we leaned against the construction barricades and took pictures of ourselves with the Brandenburg Gate in the background.

As my siblings and I were walking and talking, I noticed a man dressed like a typical West German tourist with a colorful matching jacket, pants and shoes taking pictures within earshot of us. He was the only other person in the immediate area and was very nonchalant in his demeanor. I was curious why he stood so close to us and was intent on listening to our conversation. My brother-in-law Fritz noticed this man as well.

We started out toward the Alexander Platz and he went in the same direction following several steps behind us. We stopped deliberately to let him pass. "I noticed that you have been following us," I challenged him. He denied it and said it was most certainly a coincidence. ***"Ich bin aus Köln,"*** (I am from Cologne.) he said. His dialect was believable. I told him that we would not move until he went in his own direction.

We decided to walk around the block in the opposite direction of the Cologne tourist to be sure that we didn't cross paths again. We succeeded. We now realized why it had taken me so long to cross the border. The guards had to arrange someone to trail me and watch my movement within the city. What kind of man spoke German and carried an American passport?

As it was getting near lunch and beer time, we asked one of the few pedestrians along the way for directions to the closest restaurant. Sensing that we were from the

West, he gave us directions, albeit reluctantly, to one of Berlin's oldest restaurants, ***Gasthaus zur Letzten Instanz***. We approached the restaurant with its name barely visible on the dirty stucco storefront and assumed that it wasn't busy during the lunch hour since there were no cars parked in front and only a few bicycles were parked in the rack. We were taken aback to find the place crowded with every table full. There was no background music or loud conversation in this place full of 200 people. Everyone spoke quietly and began whispering upon our entrance. All eyes turned to us because they could tell by our appearance that we came from the West.

After a brief wait, we were directed to a table that sat eight people. We asked the two men at the end of the table if we could join them. They nodded their heads affirmatively, but did not speak to us. The waitress reminded us that she could not accept payment in West German Marks unless we did an even one to one exchange. We ordered some beer and invited our tablemates to join us. They declined by saying that they had to return to work. That would have been an unbelievable excuse in the West.

The entire restaurant was so quiet you could hear a pin drop. Conversations were hushed and the men sitting beside us only watched us and listened to our conversation. Perhaps they were unfamiliar with our Swabian dialect. It was an eerie feeling knowing that all eyes and ears were on us. Once we left that depressing environment, we suddenly realized that we were the only people smiling and laughing in the entire place.

We headed again toward the ***Alexanderplatz***. Brochures advertised this central square as modern, colorful and bustling, comparable to West Berlin's ***Kurfürstendamm***. Again we were disappointed. At least the street and sidewalks leading to the square were in reasonable repair, unlike the other areas we had seen that had potholes and broken bricks everywhere. Gisela tripped on an uneven section of sidewalk and experienced a skinned knee. Now and then we noticed a few Trabants, the tiny East German two-cylinder car. The car was so inefficient that it barely reached 50 mph and it left clouds of foul-smelling exhaust in its wake.

We also noticed a group of unsmiling and passive people lined up in front of a variety store. The store was not even half full of shoppers. Yet, for crowd control, shoppers waited their turn outside the entrance. One shopper exited handing the next person a shopping basket as they then entered. We took our turn going in to this "showcase" store. We were amazed by the bare shelves and shocked at the extremely limited selection of items available for purchase.

It was a relatively warm day for mid-March so we decided to visit ***Palast der Republik*** (Palace of the Republic). This building was a combination museum and assembly hall with restaurants, small cafés and souvenir shops full of communist propaganda. We took our time looking at the exhibits, but did not buy anything. The palace was one of the few new buildings built by the communists in the early 1950s to impress the West and prove to their citizens that they could also build impressive buildings. It has since been torn down due to the lethal amount of asbestos in the building materials.

By mid-afternoon we decided to stop for coffee and dessert for the ladies and a beer for the men. The tables at the café were arranged to accommodate four guests. While we waited for a waitress, we asked the two people at the adjacent table if we could use their extra empty chairs. They answered, “We don’t know.” The waitress arrived and with hands on her hips berated us in a loud army sergeant like manner for moving the chairs. She asked us who had given us permission to move the chairs. Fritz answered that it was customary in the West to rearrange chairs at a table to accommodate more people at a table. The waitress snapped back, “Well you aren’t in the West! And furthermore, hang your coats in the closet by the entrance instead of draping them over your chairs!”

Our retort was to leave the café and go elsewhere. Realizing that there might be a party official among the customers who might turn her in to the authorities for rude behavior to tourists, she suddenly changed her posture and practically begged us to stay. And, we did.

We returned to Checkpoint Charlie at the end of the day. The guards waved us through after checking our passports again. They asked about any goods or souvenirs that we had purchased during our visit. None. For us anything we needed or wanted was better and cheaper in the West than in the East. Even the beer!

Although we experienced only 8 hours of life in the DDR, we were thrilled to return to the freedom of West Berlin. On our flight back to Stuttgart, we met the minister-president of Baden-Württemberg, Lothar Späth. He was flying coach class along with us. We exchanged greetings and shared our experience in East Berlin. Our parting words to him were, ***"Jetzt müssen wir wieder schaffen und Häusle bauen."*** (Now we need to get back to work and build a little house.) He smiled and said, ***"Ich habe von meinen schwäbischen Landsleuten nichts anderes erwartet."*** (I didn't expect anything less from my Swabian countrymen.)

Thanks to the efforts of US President Ronald Reagan, West German Chancellor Helmut Kohl and Soviet Union President Mikhail Gorbachev, the Berlin Wall fell on November 9, 1989 and Germany was reunited officially on October 3, 1990.

The current trend in education is to push high school graduates toward college. I believe that studying to become a trade journeyman is equally as valuable and possibly a better path for some students. Based on income potential, I choose and recommend the trade school route.

Both college entry and trade school require a high school diploma. A trade school education can often be completed quicker and enables the person to enter the workforce and establish a credit rating sooner. A college degree may require many more years of study, but does not always enable a graduate to achieve greater earning power over a highly skilled tradesperson or business owner.

My personal experience goes as follows: I began my Cement Mason Apprenticeship working for Uncle Gene at age 18 earning 60% of a journeyman's wage in 1952. I graduated in 1956 right before being drafted into the army in December. While in the military 1957-58, I earned $98 per month. By the time I married in May 1960, I had enough money earned and saved to make a 50% down payment on the mortgage of a $16,800 house. This would not have been possible had I gone to college.

Our son, Steve, began his Cement Mason Apprenticeship at E.L.Bulach Company in June 1979 after high school graduation. With his earnings, he was able to buy a brand new VW Scirocco and still have money in his pocket; something his college bound friends did not have. Today, he is owner of his own construction company.

It is not just the trade education that is important; it is the ability to become a competent craftsman with pride and high regard for ones own talent, skill and work. I get a great sense of satisfaction when I drive by any of our concrete projects and see the Bulach stamp with the year imprinted in a corner. I smile and think to myself, "Another job well done!" ***Handwerk hat goldenen Boden.*** (A trade in hand finds gold in every land.) And, ***Früh übt sich wer ein Meister werden will.*** (Early practice makes a master.)

During the 1980s, I was often called home to Germany because my mother was critically ill and her health was failing. My mother had been diagnosed with hemophilia in the early 1970s and was subject to frequent hemorrhages. She was missing the Rhesus factor 8 and required about 50 blood transfusions up until her death on December 8, 1988. (It is a miracle that yellow jaundice is the only other illness she acquired from the amount of transferred blood given her.)

During the last precious years of her life, I returned to Germany to be with her at least once a year. Sometimes I went twice. On many occasions she bounced back to health after a transfusion while I was visiting. My siblings thought it was because I was there beside her and the family was together again. I never heard my mother complain about her long, drawn out ordeal. She was a fighter, reinforced by her strong belief in the power of prayer and her unwavering Christian faith. In spite of her medical problems, she reached the respectable age of 83 years and 4 months.

When my father and siblings informed me of my mother's death, I booked a round-trip ticket to Stuttgart. The Christmas rush had just begun. I could get to Germany, but it was very difficult to get any type of return ticket to Minneapolis before Christmas. None of the airlines, Lufthansa, Northwest, United or American Airlines would guarantee a return ticket. Continental Airlines booked my return flight on December 23 with the understanding that a member of the Armed Forces flying home could bump me off the flight.

After my mother's funeral on December 12, I spent 10 quiet days grieving with my father, siblings and other family members. On the day of my return flight, I arrived 3 hours early at the airport in Frankfurt to be sure that my name was put on the flight manifest. According to the gate agent, I had a temporary seat assignment. With more than 2 hours before flight time, I could still be bumped from the plane. She suggested that I check with Pan Am across the concourse as they might have some open seats. Pan Am flight number 103 was departing at the same time as the Continental flight to New York, but with a scheduled stop in London. To my relief they had some open seats so I put my name on their waiting list in the event that I lost my seat on Continental.

As I left the Pan Am area, I scanned the waiting passengers to see if I recognized any familiar faces. I remember seeing many smiling, young faces full of anticipation of spending the Christmas holidays with family and friends. Many of the passengers appeared to be students. Back at the Continental gate, as I was anxiously waiting the final boarding of our aircraft, I noticed several uniformed servicemen checking in. Some came with a spouse or friends. I wondered if I would have to resort to plan B. Finally, during the final boarding call, two names were called for the last available seats. My name was one of them. I was glad to be headed home.

When I arrived home, Erné was at choir practice so I called Steve to come pick me up from the airport. On the ride home, Steve informed me that a Pan Am airplane headed for New York – JFK had crashed in Scotland just a few hours earlier. Erné had not heard the news report until Bob Galkiewicz asked her at choir when I was coming home and on what airline was I flying. He told her what he had heard on the news. Erné was beside herself with fear over the news because she knew that I could be bumped from the Continental flight and catch a flight on another airline in order to be home in time for Christmas.

Erné called Steve immediately. He assured her that I returned home safe and sound. For our family, it was a very Merry Christmas. However, for the families of the Pan Am Flight 103 victims, it was a tragic Christmas. Whenever I think about that day and the events leading up to it, I say a prayer for those innocent travelers and their families. I also say a prayer of gratitude that my life was spared and I lived to tell the story.

During our 2008 visit in Germany, Erné, Gisela, Helmut and I agreed to combine our 50th Wedding Anniversary parties. We would renew our marriage vows with a worship service at our home church in Echterdingen on Saturday, July 10, 2010 followed by a dinner reception at the locally renowned Gasthaus zum Hirsch. Pastor Neudorfer agreed to officiate the service and he was thrilled to be able to bless his first double ***Goldene Hochzeit*** (Golden Wedding Anniversary). We returned to Minnesota to begin planning and inviting our American friends to the party.

We were amazed and pleased at the positive response we had to the invitation. Friends and family planned their schedules to make the trip to Germany with great anticipation. There were 27 American guests helping to fill the church pews for the worship service to renew our marriage vows. The number of American guests present astonished the pastor and our German family and friends. Scott Fury, a former W. St. Paul neighbor, even drove 8 hours from his business trip in Amsterdam to surprise us that day.

July 10, 2010 was the warmest summer day Germany had experienced that year with a record- breaking temperature of 40°C (~104°F). The hundred-year-old stone church sanctuary was a welcome reprieve with cooler temperatures inside.

The two anniversary couples processed into the sanctuary to Beethoven's 'Ode to Joy' played by 3 trumpets with organ accompaniment. The music rang throughout the church. My eyes filled with tears at the beautiful music. Pastor Neudorfer welcomed our American guests in English, but continued the 45-minute service in German.

At the end, we all recessed from the church to the outdoor beer garden of the Hirsch, where we enjoyed refreshments and snacks before moving inside the restaurant to the upstairs dining room. There was dinner, music, speeches and conversation.

Nieces Linda and Heike presented Erné, Gisela, Helmut and me a video tribute highlighting our lives. Food and beverage, per German tradition, were plentiful. The irony of the day was that, due to the hot and humid weather, more mineral water than beer was consumed! Keep in mind that beer was cheaper than water.

Monday morning, we, Erné and Eberhard, and our American guests along with Gisela and Helmut Schwarz, Marianne Elsasser, Fritz Bulach, and Margot and Helmut Kehrer boarded a 48-seat touring bus driven by Erné's cousin Herbert Häcker with on-board service by his wife, Kathy. We were off on a 3-day bus tour of southern Germany visiting Rothenburg ob der Tauber, Berchtesgaden, The Eagle's Nest, Königssee, Augsburg and Ulm.

We were quite a jovial group. Language barriers were cast aside as everyone came together through sightseeing, meals, beer drinking, singing, storytelling and relaxing. The weather was hot, but the skies were perfectly clear for viewing the majestic splendor of the Austrian Alps and the other land- and cityscapes. Upon our return to Hotel Sonne in Echterdingen, my brother, Fritz, led his own tour through Stuttgart and to the Mercedes Benz and Porsche Museum. This much smaller group traveled by foot, bus, streetcar and ***Zahnradbahn*** (rack-railway).

Erné and I feel truly blessed by the presence of so many family and friends, who were willing to travel to Germany and our hometown for this "once in a lifetime" celebration.

'Older and Bolder' is a phrase penned on one of my birthday cards celebrating my 80th birthday. This line resonates with me especially because of the person who wrote it – Norma Rae Hunt, my pastor and spiritual mentor.

What does she mean by "bolder"? As I'm rounding third base and heading for home on my life's journey, should I continue to take chances, stick my neck out like a turtle from its shell and search for new challenges? At this new age, I feel that I have arrived at the mountaintop. Do I need to conquer new heights or gain earthly possessions? No!

Just as it did with my mother-in-law, Ecclesiastes 3:1-8 (To everything there is a season) reflects my life in its current state. I have experienced everything life and God can offer, except death. Erné has been and continues to be by my side every step of the way. I feel truly fortunate and fulfilled. I am blessed with abundant friendships and rich experience. I have experienced two countries, spoken two languages, learned a trade in both Germany and the United States, built a successful business, raised a beautiful family and earned a PhD in the school of "hard knocks" – sweat and common sense. Life is complete and I am content.

APPENDIX

EBERHARD'S TIMELINE

1934	April 24 - Eberhard born in Stuttgart, Germany First son of Fritz and Emma Bulach
1939	Sept 1 - Germany invades Poland, start of WWII
1945	May 8 - end of WWII in Europe
1948	Began apprenticeship as a machinist
1951	October 10 - arrived in New York City, NY October 14 - arrived in St. Paul, MN
1957	Drafted into the U.S. Army
1958	Obtained U.S. Citizenship
1959	January 18 - Honorable Discharge from U.S. Army
1960	May 28 - married Erné Kehrer (b. March 1, 1940)
1961	September 4 - birth of Steven Mark Bulach
1964	April 1 - began E.L.Bulach Company November 5 - birth of Kristina Jean Bulach
1972	Formed B&L Co., purchased construction yard, purchased Bomanite license.
1995	Formed Bulach Development and moved into new office building Moved residence from W. St. Paul to Sunfish Lake
2004	Steven Bulach assumes leadership of E.L.Bulach Co.
2014	Moved to senior housing at The Villas of Lilydale
2016	Dissolved Bulach Development
2018	September 30 - complete retirement
2020	March 1 - celebrate Erné's 80th birthday
2020	May 28 - 60th Anniversary celebration delayed due to COVID-19 pandemic

EBERHARD'S TEN COMMANDMENTS OF SUCCESS

1. WORK HARD & SMART

Hard work is the best investment and habit a person can attain. Think and observe everything while you work.

2. STUDY HARD

Knowledge enables everyone to work more effectively.

3. TAKE INITIATIVE

Get out of a rut. Be a "Self Starter". Believe in your own ability. Take the road less travelled.

4. LOVE YOUR WORK

Only then will you find satisfaction in mastering it.

5. BE A PERFECTIONIST

Slipshod methods bring slipshod results. However, don't let failure discourage you from trying again.

6. APPRECIATE CONQUEST

This is payback for all the challenges in achieving your dream.

7. CULTIVATE PERSONALITY

Lead by example with a positive attitude.

8. HELP/ SHARE WITH OTHERS

Greatness lies in giving opportunity to others.

9. BE DEMOCRATIC

As a leader or a follower, always be fair.

10. ALWAYS DO YOUR BEST

Be focused on, determined in, and responsible for your actions!

ENDNOTES

1 The song 'America' is the most fitting and condensed version of my (Eberhard) dream and life's journey.

2 The war in Europe ended May 8, 1945, V-E Day (Victory in Europe). For those of us living in Echterdingen, the war was over on April 25, 1945 when our town was occupied by the French forces.

3 After immigrating to the U.S., I learned that rations were also common there, too. The items rationed in the US were meat, sugar, gas, tires, cigarettes, whiskey, butter and even bubble gum.

4 In those days, plastic bags and wrapping paper did not exist. Shoppers carried their purchases home in their own baskets and furnished their own wrapping paper, which was usually yesterday's newspaper.

5 ***Jungvolk*** was for boys 10-14 years old. ***Hitler Jugend*** was for boys 15-18 years old. There are many books and movies about the Hitler Youth Movement and its rookie organization, ***Deutsches Jungvolk***.

6 Streetlights were not lit at night. Our curtains and blinds were drawn tightly so the smallest ray of light could not escape into the night and give the enemy aircraft a target for bombing.

7 A man-made lake formed by a huge excavation for clay that provided raw materials for a nearby brick factory.

8 Clothing articles were rationed during the war just like everything else. Since our growing bodies changed from year to year, families were allowed to purchase a new uniform every two years — if they were available.

[9] The potato bug is similar in shape to the American June bug, but is twice as big with black and green stripes across its back. The skeleton is so hard that the bugs can only be destroyed by burning, being run over with cars or hit with a hammer.

[10] Filder-Zeitung, Freitag, 15. März 2019, "Der Luftkrieg lässt die Bilder in Flammen aufgehen," von Rüdiger Ott und Eileen Breuer, 75 year anniversary issue of the bombing of Echterdingen.

[11] POWs were considered expendable in the event of an air raid. Their labor was used to fix the bomb craters on the runways and any roads, especially thc autobahn, from March 1944 - May 1945.

[12] Christian Social Union Party and Free Democratic Party.

[13] Statistics taken from the U.S. Bureau of Labor Statistics https://www.bls.gov/opub/ted/2011/ted_20111011.htm and Statista https://www.statista.com/statistics/375209/unemployment-rate-in-germany/

[14] Statistics taken from the Country Economy website https://countryeconomy.com/gdp?year=1965

[15] Herbert Clark Hoover, 31st President of the United States and president during the Great Depression 1929-1933. Not to be confused with J. Edgar Hoover, longtime head of the FBI from 1924-1972.

[16] Boswell, James, "The Ominous Years 1774-1776", edited by Charles Ryskamp and Frederick A. Pottle, McGraw-Hill, New York, 1963, p. 291 (23 March 1776).

[17] Filder-Zeitung, Freitag, 15. März 2019, "Der Luftkrieg lässt die Bilder in Flammen aufgehen," von Rüdiger Ott und Eileen Breuer, photo originally from Landesvermessungsamt (Land Survey Office).

[18] Since we did not have a bathtub or a shower at home, I took care of my bathing needs in the very modern and up-to-date bathrooms and showering facilities at work before heading home. Most of my other co-workers did the same.

[19] Ruth Degler, daughter of Fritz Degler and Frieda (née Bulach) Degler, sister of Fritz and Eugene Bulach. She was orphaned as a toddler and adopted by her maternal uncle and his wife, Eugene and Florence Bulach.

[20] General Motors, Ford and Chrysler.

[21] Due to a manpower shortage, the prison guards were POWs from Poland and other Easter European countries captured early in the war by the Germans. These men were promised better treatment, safety, food and even nominal payment for their services. They had rifles without live ammunition. The other POWs took advantage of this when they learned about that.

[22] The MS Gripsholm was a Swedish ocean liner chartered by the US government after WWII as an exchange and repatriation ship for Japanese and German nationals sailing under the auspices of the International Red Cross. The ship was sold to Norddeutscher Lloyd in 1954 and renamed the MS Berlin.

[23] A person who carries the company flag in front of the marching formation.

[24] Although there was an unwritten code among recruits never to volunteer for anything, I learned that volunteering for a special detail or duty was usually beneficial throughout my military career. I felt that the jobs came with a challenge for me to do my best.

[25] No automatic or assault weapons were issued at that time. We received only 5 rounds of ammunition in a single clip.

[26] These Quads were made famous by Burt Lancaster in the movie "From Here to Eternity" where he fires at an attacking Japanese airplane from one of the barrack rooftops.

[27] From 1957-58, the second Formosa or Taiwan Strait Crisis put the U.S. on high alert. John Foster Dulles, U.S. Secretary of State at the time, had several units of the 25th Division practice getting on and off troop ships in Pearl Harbor should an emergency arise. Thank God the crisis fizzled and none of us had to put our jungle warfare skills to use.

[28] Nabuo Miamoto was a member of the 442 Regimental Combat Team composed of Japanese Americans. It was the most decorated U.S. army unit during WWII. They fought in the battles of Anzio and Monte Casino at great odds against the German army. The parents and siblings of some of these men were actually sent to internment camps in California. Nabuo had the rank of E-7 master sergeant.

[29] In an emergency, Tripler could handle 3,000 patients.

[30] Names of traditional German clothing.

[31] Armistice Day (also known as Veterans' Day): 11:00am on November 11, 1918. The Allied powers signed a ceasefire agreement with Germany bringing the war (now known as WWI) to an end.

[32] A bedroll and bunk were provided at the airport terminal for military service personnel staying overnight.

[33] Diapers were washed and hung to air-dry overnight in the cool air of the attic. They froze stiff and straight!

[34] "In wine there is wisdom, in beer there is freedom, in water there is bacteria." Original quote by Benjamin Franklin.

[35] Paraphrased from the Merriam-Webster Dictionary. http://www.merriam-webster.com/dictionary/liberty.

[36] 'Sailor Linked to First WWII Shot Honored' by Michael M. Phillips, Wall Street Journal, Thursday, May 21, 2015, Vol. CCLXV No. 118.